Palgrave Studies in Prisons and Penology

This is a unique and innovative series, the first of its kind dedicated entirely to prison scholarship. At a historical point in which the prison population has reached an all-time high, the series seeks to analyse the form, nature and consequences of incarceration and related forms of punishment. Palgrave Studies in Prisons and Penology provides an important forum for burgeoning prison research across the world.

More information about this series at
http://www.palgrave.com/gp/series/14596

Nahid Rahimipour Anaraki

Prison in Iran

A Known Unknown

palgrave
macmillan

Nahid Rahimipour Anaraki
Memorial University
St. John's, NL, Canada

Palgrave Studies in Prisons and Penology
ISBN 978-3-030-57168-9 ISBN 978-3-030-57169-6 (eBook)
https://doi.org/10.1007/978-3-030-57169-6

This Palgrave Macmillan imprint is published by the registered company Springer Nature Switzerland AG.
The registered company address is: Gewerbestrasse 11, 6330 Cham, Switzerland

Acknowledgments

This work would not have been possible without inspiration, guidance, support, and encouragement of various individuals who I have had a chance to meet in my life. These individuals' tireless dedication to my work has made this manuscript possible. It is difficult to name all of them and their valuable contributions in the process of completing this work.

First and foremost, I would like to express my sincere appreciation to Dr. Anton Oleinik, whose confidence in me made this study possible. There are few people who understand better than him how much energy has been devoted to this study. Dr. Oleinik was the first who encouraged me to publish this research as a book and also the first who read and provided me with valuable suggestions on early draft of the manuscript. I am grateful for his generous support and the freedom he granted me during this journey. I would also like to thank Dr. Masoud Kianpour and Dr. Jennifer Selby, who served as members of my dissertation committee and provided me with helpful comments.

I want to express my appreciation to my participants who shared their lives, pains, spiritual transformations, and experiences with me and agreed to be part of this journey. Those participants, many of whom were considered "unwanted" in the society, assisted me in bringing out and expressing their forgotten and denied humanity. Many of the participants of this study were enduring the intolerable pains of drug abuse or terrible prison conditions, yet they assisted me with open hearts.

Many close friends and mentors deserve mention, particularly those who made significant contributions in the process of data gathering and linking me to the various gatekeepers in governmental and non-governmental organizations throughout Iran and those who provided me with accommodation and transportation while traveling in different cities. Friends include but are not limited to Nima Emamian, Akbar Emamian, Mona Dehghan, Arastoo Bozorgi, Rasoul Vaezipour, and Sardar Sohrabi. A special note of appreciation to Samaneh Ghasemi Tabatabaei, my best friend whose support during data collection in Tehran will not be forgotten. Much of my research skills came from working with Dr. Siamak Zand Razavi and Dr. Dariush Boostani. I am grateful to them for educating, supporting, and inspiring me.

No acknowledgment would be complete without recognizing the unwavering patience and unconditional support of my family, Shadi, Shohre, Javad, Farshid, Kian, and Shahnaz. Their continued support and encouragement are greatly appreciated. I would like to give special thanks to my mom and dad, Sadiye and Ali, who have been always next to me while I was wandering along the various paths of my life. This work would not have been possible without a financial support of my dad; his kindness, generosity, and tolerance remain with me forever. Thank you all.

Contents

List of Figures

List of Tables

1

Introduction

The So-Called Prison

In the summer of 2012, after receiving a call from the manager of a non-governmental childcare organization in Iran, I became the principal investigator of a research team, which teamed up with the prison in one of the most populated cities in the Islamic Republic of Iran to run a prison's kindergarten. After various meetings and background checks, I received official permission to get access to the women's ward. Every Tuesday and Thursday morning in the hot summer of 2012, I went to the prison with a black chador and no makeup to collect data. The bus route that went straight to the prison was not always crowded with people; there was a bus stop across the street from the prison entrance. Whenever I got off the bus at the stop, other passengers looked at me strangely. Considering prisoners as "dangerous" and "bad" people who have to be kept inside the walls since they are not capable or deserving of living like ordinary citizens is a pervasive stereotype in Iranian society. I, as a researcher working in prison, received several puzzled comments and questions from people: How can you dare to sit and talk with prisoners?

N. R. Anaraki, *Prison in Iran*, Palgrave Studies in Prisons and Penology,
https://doi.org/10.1007/978-3-030-57169-6_1

Are you scared when you talk with the murderers? How can you talk with them for six hours? Are there children inside the prison?

I remember the day when one of the incarcerated mothers wanted to give up her baby girl since the mother was on a death row. The non-governmental organization took responsibility to find a caregiver for the baby girl instead of sending her to a welfare organization. When some potential adopters heard about the baby girl's background, they changed their minds: she was in prison and her mother was a murderer. If one suggested her as a potential baby to adopt, they took it as an offence. This reveals the very sad reality behind the life of prisoners. The ordinary citizens do not consider them as "human." It gets even worse when their children are affected by imprisonment. They suffer the same pains and injuries. Most of the comments made by my interlocutors outside the prison walls were accompanied by smirks, hesitation, and wonder. Who are those prisoners? What are they doing in the prison? What are the children doing in and in connection with the prison?

Anyway, after going through different security checks, from one building to the next, one corridor to the next, and one room to another, I entered a big yard that was surrounded by multiple doors. One of those doors was the entrance of the "*band-e nesvan*" (women's ward). Whenever I knocked the door to go through the final security check, the women guard acted as if she had not seen me before, did not know me, and had no idea what I was doing there; some days, she even tried hard to not let me in. After going through all those security checks, which took approximately 20 to 30 minutes, I entered the women's ward. Women with colorful clothes but with the same gray color chador were in the yard. There was a store in the yard where they could buy food, fruits, clothes, and so on. I spent several months among them. I wore a black chador, which was a sign of being an "ordinary" person in the prison, an outsider; thus, all prisoners knew I was there to conduct research. Gradually, I started to be considered a trustworthy person in the prison by prisoners and by some guards (i.e. not all of them, but at least two out of the six guards). During the very first days of interviewing, one guard was always around me and even tried to overhear the conversations between me and the inmates. However, the trust between me as a researcher and some guards was built gradually. Most often, I spent an entire day with prisoners, and could even visit other sections of the prison such as the library, social workers' offices, and visiting rooms.

After getting familiar with some of the prisoners and listening to their painful stories, I did not feel like I was an outsider. At some of the times in the prison, I thought I was one of them, and they felt the same. They felt much more comfortable with sharing their stories. However, the guards several times warned me not to trust the prisoners at all. I was not allowed to take my phone and bag into the prison. Guards always searched me to make sure I did not have anything else but my audio recorder. I was not allowed to buy anything for anyone in the prison, even for children. One day, two sisters who were 10 and 12 and had been imprisoned for drug dealing asked me to buy a coke and fruit leather for them. They did not have money to afford such "luxuries" in the prison. Apparently, they were watching TV the night before and one of the inmates was drinking a coke and eating chips and fruit leather. I was not allowed to buy anything for the inmates, and the guards and social workers would not either. The guards were extremely sensitive about the information that might be collected by me from the sisters. Once, when the sisters and I were starting to talk, one guard came, interrupted us, and asked me about the topic we were talking about and the reason why I was talking with them. Although I conducted interviews with them at the end, the guards watched me carefully to prevent any contact between the prisoners and me.

It is important to keep in mind that obtaining official permission to access prison for me as a female researcher in 2012 could not have been possible without the full support of the NGO, which played a critical role in managing the kindergarten inside the women's division in the prison. This cooperation, which brought huge benefits for the prison as a governmental organization, provided an opportunity for me as a researcher to gain access to the prison. This, however, was not my last chance to come in contact with prisoners, as, in the summer of 2017, I traveled to Iran after years of studying and living in Canada. In 2017, even though I had several connections with NGOs, I could not access the prison. The initial group of study participants, in the summer of 2017, was recruited in different ways, each with its own limitations. To access as many subjects as possible, several requests were sent to different organizations and institutions from governmental to non-governmental. Those attempts were met with silence, so while I was waiting for a response, I sent other requests to other institutions in different locations, either in person, by phone, by email, or through gatekeepers. Different responses from different organizations were received, most of which were negative and discouraging. Most institutions, even non-governmental organizations, wrote back or called back asking for official permission from a university in Iran, and once they realized I was a female researcher who was a student in a Western country planning to do research in Iran, they did not even answer my phone calls. When communication over phone was futile, I traveled from Isfahan to different cities (446 km to Tehran, 715 km to Mazandaran, 676 km to Kerman) to consider all other opportunities. In some organizations, especially the governmental ones, I did not dare disclose the fact that I was a researcher who was studying in a Western university.[1]

At this point, I changed my strategy and negotiated with some judges who were trying to develop academic research regarding incarceration issues and who could grant access to prisoners. Also, access to incarcerated individuals was frequently provided through released prisoners, who informed me about inmates who were on leave and put me in contact with them, and there were some concerned officers working at prison who tried to help through providing interested prisoners with phone calls to conduct phone interviews (those phone interviews were canceled because of potential security issues that might threaten the researcher). Additionally, based on my previous contact with prisoners' families, in 2012, I knew some local gatekeepers who had trusting relationships with released or on-leave drug-related prisoners. Gatekeepers were approached to explain the project to any interested former prisoners.

---

[1] According to the written and unwritten rules of each of those organizations, I had to manage my dress. When visiting most governmental organizations, I wore a *chador*. I also did not wear makeup at the governmental organizations and even changed my way of speaking, using specific titles; instead of using "Mr." to refer to a man in those organizations, I used *hajj-agha*. However, when I had a meeting with a non-governmental organization's manager in Tehran, different, sometimes opposite, dress codes were required. Even in one of the night drop-in centers in south of Tehran, I was advised to wear nail polish or makeup to make my appearance more similar to the clients of those centers, and they did not consider me as an "outsider" who wants to observe and monitor them like the people from governmental agencies.

During my journey to Iran, I was warned of the potential risks of conducting research in Iran, particularly as a female student studying abroad. However, during the years of doing research on prisons in Iran, which included several visits to prison and governmental and non-governmental institutions, I did not face any serious problem with the authorities. Yes, I was reminded and warned several times both in governmental and non-governmental organizations about discussing highly sensitive topics and publishing the results; nevertheless, no explicit threat was made.

Since the topic of the research was sensitive, the critical access I had to the participants and organizations could not have been possible without struggling with the "nuance of power" (Skeggs, 1992, p. 14, cited by Malloch 2000). Accessing the field of study, especially prisons in Iran, is not only highly challenging, especially for sociologists and anthropologists, but also risky. Prisons as a field of study are always monitored by intelligence officers and the security apparatus, which makes researchers often reluctant to choose this topic. However, there is a popular genre of prison literature in Iran, which was started by the novel entitled *Prison Scrap Papers* written by Bozorg Alavi. His book depicts, through real and fictional characters and events, the daily life of prisoners locked up inside the walls and how they try to maintain their dignity, privacy, and political convictions. Several prison memoirs have been published since then, and the number significantly increased after the 1979 revolution. The memoirs have been written mostly by political and social activists who survived the prisons. Those books provide a wealth of information about the conditions of prisons in Iran before and after the revolution. Nevertheless, the dearth of scholarly work on prisons in Iran—both in this country and in the West—was a major motivation behind this book. Hence, its title—**A Known Unknown**[2]—is not simply a figure of speech. We simply do not know much about Iranian prisons while they certainly exist and their operation has a significant impact of lives of many people: prisoners, members of their families, especially children, and prison guards.

[2] There is no connection with Rumsfeld's argument, for the sake of clarity (his original argument on the terrorist threat as the "unknown unknown" was made at a news briefing of February 12, 2002, see https://archive.defense.gov/Transcripts/Transcript.aspx?TranscriptID=2636).

The best way to shed light on the prisoners' life is through their own voices.[3] Their stories unmask the severity of the pain they suffer in the prison. The stories also reveal the prisoners and children's constant struggles to survive the intolerable conditions inside and outside the prison. There is virtually no research that addresses the dilemma of incarcerated mothers and the experiences of their children. This book presents the voices of incarcerated women and men. They are stigmatized as whores, bad parents, useless, addicts, and trash.

This study was conducted in two different settings[4]: governmental organizations (e.g. compulsory drug treatment camps,[5] the Association for the Protection of Prisoners, Court, prisons, voluntary drug treatment camps) and non-governmental organizations (e.g. Narcotics Anonymous, the Sun House women's rehabilitation center (see Fig. 1.1), the night drop-in center in Tehran (see Figs. 1.2 and 1.3), the Rebirth Charity Society, located in four cities (Isfahan, Kerman, Mazandaran, Tehran) of the Islamic Republic of Iran. The participants included 38 males and 52 females (22 of women participants have been recruited in 2017 and 30 have been recruited in 2012) aged 10–65 years who were on leave at the time of the interview (5 participants), being released (1 participant), incarcerated and on their court day (4 participants), in prison (30 participants), in compulsory camps (3 participants), in mother and child centers (7 participants), in night drop-in centers (4 participants), in rehabilitation centers (5 participants), in voluntarily camps (10 participants), a wanted criminal (1 participant), and in Narcotics Anonymous (20 participants). Almost all were Muslim; and one was Christian. Most

[3] For this reason, I utilized Grounded Theory (GT) in my research. Therefore, participants' experiences, understandings, and perceptions about their lives have been central when conducting in-depth, semi-structured, and open-ended interviews.

[4] The field work was approved by Memorial's Research Ethics Board and was performed in accordance with TCSP (Canada's Tri-Council Policy Statement: Ethical Conduct for Research Involving Humans).

[5] The compulsory treatment camps (state-run camps) as governmental institutions were designed to lock arrested "street" and "homeless" addicts into a treatment environment instead of incarceration, to force them to quit drugs. Most addicts are collected through the large gathering programs ("purifying plan") on the streets and will be subsequently sent to the compulsory camps. Those camps make the violence against people who use drugs more "private" and "invisible" compared with prison. In the name of treatment and having a "healthier" society, especially in specific areas of the cities, the compulsory and forced treatment centers regulate and control people who use drugs.

Fig. 1.1 People who use drugs consume and exchange drugs in the street close to the women's rehabilitation center Sun House, Tehran. Photo by the author, 2017

participants reported the age of onset of abusing drugs as between 10 and 18 years old; however, 6 participants noted that they had begun abusing drugs between the ages 7 and 9. Their crimes were mostly related to illegal drugs (e.g. some were incarcerated for possessing illegal drugs, some for abusing drugs, some for drug trafficking, and some for committing murder while high on drugs).[6]

[6] The so-called war on drugs or anti-drug campaign in the Islamic Republic of Iran has had irreversible and unexpected consequences since 1979, with drug users being considered a "danger" and a "national threat," which has legitimized mass executions and incarcerations. In 1979, the Islamic Revolution in Iran brought to power the radical conservative Islamists, under the leadership of the supreme leader, Ayatollah Ruhollah Khomeini. The leader of the Islamic Revolution in Iran declared that the consumption and trafficking of illicit drugs in the Islamic Republic of Iran is a direct result of the influence of Western culture and should be prohibited (Ghiabi 2015). Today, the regime remains dominated by a conservative group and another supreme leader, Ayatollah Ali Khamenei. Drug-related offenders still receive large fines, lengthy sentences, corporal punishment, and, in some cases, the death penalty (e.g. 21 executions in one week of January 2014). The number of those incarcerated for drug-related offences has been rising sharply, from 101,801 in 1993, to 204,385 in 2010, and 217,851 in 2014. However, the capacity of Iran's prisons was only 113,000 in 2012 (IHRDC, 2015). It has been well documented that approximately 60% of prisoners in Iran are incarcerated due to drug-related crimes; over 80,000 drug-related offenders were arrested in 2000, and this number increased to 314,268 in 2007 (Calabrese 2007; Nissaramanesh,

Fig. 1.2 Night drop-in centre in Tehran. Photo by the author, 2017

Fig. 1.3 Night drop-in centre in Tehran. Photo by the author, 2017

In Iran, the public spectacle of torturing has not disappeared yet, as public executions and floggings still occur. Punishment is not a hidden dimension of the Islamic penal system. The objective of this book is not to study torture in Iran, rather to explore the painful lives of prisoners and their families—"collateral" victims who were affected by the legal system with no just cause. There are some informative books about torture in Iran, including *Tortured Confessions* (1999) by Edvard Abrahamian and *Torture and Modernity* (1994) by Darius M. Rejali, each of which significantly inspired me in different ways. However, this book uncovers the conditions of so-called prisons in Iran. This book aims to depict Iranian prisons in a way that is different from that explained in Foucault's *Discipline and Punish*. Modernizing the buildings and referring to them as prisons does not imply an institutional transformation; in other words, only the architectural design has changed significantly compared to the situation 50 years ago. Generally speaking, punitive practices have not changed significantly in Iran during the last decades. Although some efforts have been made to adjust the penal system in Iran based on the new moralities, as Katouzian (2004) put it, everything has a short-term nature in Iranian society in which all changes, even fundamental ones, tended to have short-term consequences only, making all efforts like a "pick-axe building."[7] The penal history of Iran has never experienced "the age of sobriety in punishment" and "a slackening of the hold on the body" (Foucault 1979, pp. 14–10). While it is believed that prison is not just "a mere loss of liberty" and that a "trace of torture" even in the modern penal system is inevitable, "a mere torture" constitutes the distinctive

Trace, & Roberts, 2005). According to Iran Human Rights (IHR) and ECPM (Together Against the Death Penalty) (2016, p. 16), "more than 2,990 people were executed on drug offences between 2010 and 2016." In 2011, more than 509 drug-related offenders were executed, and this number decreased to 296 in 2016. However, Iran has ranked second in the world for the number of executions carried out annually, with two-thirds of the executions for drug-related crimes ranging from minor offences (e.g. transportation of more than 30 grams of narcotics) to major offences (e.g. armed smuggling) (Gallahue, P. and Lines, R. 2015; Hlinomaz et al. 2014).

[7] "Most of these buildings are no more than 30 (even 20) years old, and they are normally sound in foundation and structure. In a few cases they may be run down and in need of renovation, but the feature that results in their condemnation as such, incidentally wipes off the value of the structure and only leaves the price of their site, is that their architecture and/or interior design is unfashionable according to the latest forms, concepts or whims. Thus, rather than build a new house or whatever, thus adding to the stock of existing physical capital, it is demolished by the owner or purchaser, and a new building is erected on its sit" (Katouzian 2004, pp. 1–2).

feature of Iranian prisons. Although the penal severity has been reduced, it has also extended and now includes not just prisoners but also their families, regardless of their age and gender. In Iran, penalties still target the body, but now also affect the bodies of whole family. It is not just prisoners who suffer from the lack of food, clothes, spaces for sleeping, health services, legal services, safety, and threats of physical violence and abuse, but also their families. The penal system in Iran might not be in the "bodiless reality" but is definitely in the "bodiless illusion," and a few rehabilitation and educational programs, social skills training sessions, and alternatives to prison could not shake the apparatus of the punitive system. It is not accurate to simply admit that the system aims to treat criminals, obtain a cure for criminality, and provide training and correct their behavior with the help of the few techniques and scientific discourses in the penal system of Iran. Of course, one might say that there are some intentions, but they are not serious. In *Discipline and Punish*, Foucault describes the transition from torture to imprisonment in the West, and he considered prisons as a novel way of exercising power. Instead of exercising power through torture, discipline becomes a means of governance, and prisons are one of the manifestations of the new age of governing and disciplining. What I intend to make clear is that torture as a technique for exercising power over the body is nested in the so-called prison and targets the lives of prisoners in their cells along with the bodies of their families outside the prison. This type of governing people departs from public executions and ceremonial processions. It operates in the visiting rooms of children with mothers, in a long line of distributing methadone in prisons, in the bodies of mothers in labor behind the closed doors of a cell, and in the eyes of ten-year-old girls in prison. Although the lives of prisoners are not comparable with those who are living outside, prisoners and their families are sharing the same injuries and pains caused by imprisonment.

Chapter two provides an overview of the history of prisons, the penal system as well as prison conditions during three periods in Iran: the Qajar, Pahlavi, and the Islamic Revolution in 1979. The main technique used to exercise power in Qajar society was torture, focusing on the bodies on the public scaffold. A combination of religious, unstructured, unwritten, despotic, and arbitrary laws laid the groundwork for "the gloomy festival of punishment." Criminals were kept in either governmental or private prisons, and the state was not seen to be responsible for providing for the essential needs of either. Criminals were either buried alive or became an actor of the "horror execution theatre" in public. The body of laws was shaken drastically during 1905–1909 by the Constitutional Revolution, the draft of Islamic law was reviewed based on the French penal code, the Special Criminal Court was established in Tehran in 1917, a discourse against ceremonial punishments flourished, juridical torture was banned, and executions were restricted to hanging or firing squads. Prison conditions, however, did not change significantly. Prisoners in prison number one in Tehran, which was referred to as a "dark prison" or *Siah Chal* (dark hole), had no beds, fresh air, or light. In 1925, Reza Shah, the founder of the Pahlavi dynasty, made several efforts to overhaul the traditional legal system by reforming the penal code and separating it from the Islamic roots by relying on the European legal tradition; however, the roots of Islamic principles were still traceable. Also, as a result of the growing number of prisoners and the insufferable prison conditions, a large number of prisons in 34 cities with modern facilities were established during Reza Shah's reign. One of these was Qasr prison in Tehran, which was opened in 1929. As Abrahamian (1999, p. 27) states, "Qasr become a notorious symbol of the Pahlavi state and the new judicial system." An inseparable part of the penal system in Iran from the Qajar to the Pahlavi reign was exercising power over bodies; however, this became much more explicit, brutal, and sophisticated from 1971 to 1977 as a result of the systematic use of sophisticated interrogation techniques. By the end of 1975, the regime was overwhelmed by international human rights organizations' criticism and was forced to ban torture and release the majority of prisoners. In 1979, after the Islamic Revolution, Ayatollah Khomeini, "made it an absolute to turn the prison into an educational institution, where the Islam and Revolution dominant" (Carlsen 1982, pp. 147–148). Now, with prisoners under the control of the Revolutionary guards, not much has changed, as the widespread use of torture in Iranian prisons has put the Islamic Republic of Iran under the severe criticism of human rights organizations. As a result, prison conditions were improved as a result of adapting measures ranging from releasing some prisoners to lifting restrictions on reading some non-religious books. However, between 1980 and 1986, every two minutes, one person was incarcerated, and in less than six years, the population of prisons increased by 91% due to the growing number of political prisoners and the enforcement of the laws on drug-related crimes. Finally, as a result of emphasizing on punishment rather than correction, the same story was seen as in the previous decades. Prisons turned into "criminal universities."

The third chapter depicts the subculture of current Iranian prisons through seven categories: (1) unstable pyramid, (2) captive as a society, (3) battle zone, (4) hegemony of drug-related networks, (5) multiple identities, (6) instrumental relationships, and (7) two sides of the same coin. The first section of this chapter demonstrates the instability of prison society. The main goal of a prison code is the maintenance of prison solidarity and cohesion. Thus, the more the inmates follow the prison code, the more the stability and solidarity between prisoners is guaranteed. When this code breaks down, a "war of all against all" becomes inevitable. This section explains how in Iranian prisons, adopting informal rules simultaneously fosters solidarity and instability. The second section focuses on deprivation as a common characteristic of prisons around the world; however, this was not the case of Iranian prisons. Violent criminals, especially drug traffickers (called "prison kings"), use their resources to create palaces inside the prison. Having privacy in a total institution requires a criminal history, economic capital, and social capital within the penal world. The third section explores fighting and using physical violence to obtain a certain degree of safety in the inmate world. Iranian prison subculture in Iran is affected to a great extent by the hegemony of prison drug networks, which is examined in the fourth section. Drugs are considered an opportunity to exercise power over the daily life of prisoners. Prisoners are provided with opportunities to consume or sell drugs, which, in turn, makes it easier for those in power (i.e. the managers of prisons) to recognize, categorize, and identify prisoners and control them. The social behaviors of these prisoners revolve around drugs, and their functionality rests on drugs. Therefore, instead of managing prisoners by employing educated correctional officers and rehabilitation programs, managers of prisoners rely on drugs as a multitasking tool. In the next section, the recriminalization process due to a lack of meaningful rehabilitation programs in the prison is explained. When rehabilitation and treatment are not priorities, prisoners focus on entertaining themselves to survive their experiences. The most popular forms of entertainment are consuming drugs and bragging about their criminal skills and escapades. The next section emphasizes the role of gangs in the prisons. Gangs in prisons are instrumental in relationships with fellow prisoners. The control of a prison depends on the number of violent criminals in each gang. Being a gang member resembles living on a safe ship in a stormy sea. Being a member of a gang brings identification, a sense of belonging, and status in prison, and it provides members with psychological and emotional support. The final section reveals the function of pseudo-correctional officers. High-status inmates are often recruited by correctional officers to control, monitor, and manage the prison. They act as pseudo-correctional officers to mitigate violence, which might otherwise disrupt the prison's social system. While trust is generally an unstable phenomenon in the penal world, correctional officers trust prisoners who exert influence and power throughout the prison to maintain that trust. Since drug traffickers have the greatest influence over others, they are the best targets for correctional officers in managing the prison.

In the fourth chapter, it is not my intention to provide historical details on Iranian women's imprisonment. Instead, I use the current historical period to demonstrate the costs of mothers' incarceration for their families, especially children. They carry the pains of imprisonment, whether they are inside the mother-child cell, in the child welfare system, homeless, runaways from home, or living with an addicted father. Children are injured by the poverty, lack of food, lack of health care systems, abusive alternative family environment, unsafe and dangerous neighborhoods, and difficulties with visiting their mothers. Although children residing with the parents in prison have benefits for both children and their parents, especially if they are equipped with mother-child facilities and programs, many are still vehemently against the idea. This multilayered opposition mostly relates to the child's well-being. However, it is not my intention to indicate my support or opposition regarding keeping children in prison. Rather, I aim to reveal the impact of incarceration on mothers and children. It is difficult to determine whether mothers' incarceration is more punishing for mothers or children. While the mother-child interactions were affected by the security environment, those who were separated from their mothers struggled with other issues, which makes it necessary to consider if the mother's incarceration also implies the child's punishment. After many years, I could never come to a decision on whether parenting in prison is more beneficial for children than parenting from prison. Obviously, it is impossible to answer this controversial question without evaluating mother-child programs in prisons. However, I had another objective in this study: to broaden the knowledge on the impacts of prison on offenders and their children. The so-called forgotten victims of the imprisonment (Robertson 2007; Codd 1998), the "invisible group" (Losel et al. 2012; Martynowicz 2011; Macbride 2008), or the "unseen victims of the prison boom" (Petersilia 2005), who are the most "visible" and "available" victims of imposing power over women, suffer extreme risks and harmful consequences due to their mothers' incarceration whether they are inside or outside prison. All the movements of children and infants that reside with mothers in prison are monitored and regulated by the guidelines and decisions of the authorities. Regulations on the times when children can go to kindergarten, when they can go in the yard, when they can eat, when they can visit family members, what they can eat, and what they can play with have the impact on all aspects of their life. I emphasize that despite all the benefits of living with children in prisons for incarcerated mothers, their motherhood and womanhood needs were deafeningly ignored. More precisely, they have not received any legal support to arrange their children's custody or birth certificates. Additionally, as addressed previously, there are no mother-child programs or training to help maternal bonding available. The situation was even worse for mothers who left their children outside the walls, as they did not expect to receive any financial or legal support to deal with the numerous social, financial, and emotional issues they face as the primary caregiver of their children. Not all incarcerated mothers are a sole parent, but inmates' partners who are not legally married could not visit the mother and child in the prison. Couples with an unregistered marriage or *sighe* (i.e. temporary marriage) were almost overwhelmed with sadness and frustration as a result of not being able to visit each other. Consequently, incarcerated mothers, even those who were not a sole caregiver, gradually became a primary and sole caregiver of the children and were overwhelmed by the responsibilities and obligations of upbringing children either in or outside prison. The question of how this burden affects mothers and children has not been taken seriously. There were no mother-child programs or training available to define and redefine their roles as a mother. In fact, the only reason for keeping children with mothers in prison was to control at least some prisoners by keeping them busy with their children. In other words, instead of monitoring incarcerated women through methadone or other sorts of drugs that were smuggled into the prison, children emerged as a more sufficient tool of control given that there were no programs and facilities available to emotionally, legally, and financially support the mother/child. What is a better option than using those innocent children to keep women busy? When there are no meaningful training programs in the prison to facilitate parenting from the prison or inside the prison, then it would be an efficient mechanism to control mothers through motherhood and make them overwhelmed and frustrated with parenting responsibilities. Meanwhile, children were tortured like criminals along with others regardless of their age and whether they were in or outside the prison. As long as punishment is the dominant discourse of the penal system, the minds and bodies of whomever are around incarcerated offenders will be tortured and remain under tremendous strain.

Being a mother and raising children in/from prison is one of the most significant differences between men and women's prison experience in addition to being involved in familial groups instead of gangs, spreading rumors instead of physical violence, and so on. In 2014, incarcerated women represented approximately 8.8 per 100,000 members of the national population, or 3.1% of the total prison population. Although this is a relatively small number compared to men, the willingness to portray the lived experiences of women in prison and the devotion of a full chapter to their situation in prison is not just due to the noteworthy differences between women and men's prison life; rather, women's conditions in the Islamic Republic of Iran play a crucial role in the victimization, isolation, and exclusion of incarcerated women. Being incarcerated, living under severe surveillance, being called a whore or troublemaker, and being excluded and isolated are a norm for women in prison. Iran is a patriarchal society (Shayestehkhou et al. 2008; Moallem 2005) characterized by a high sensitivity to women's behaviors. I devoted one chapter to women who have been consistently manipulated and abused due to gender discrimination prevailing in Iran, to depict not only their tortured bodies inside prison but also their tortured souls in the society. Further, some articles of the Islamic Law further strengthen and protect gender discrimination in general and in the system of justice in particular.[8] According to Smart and Brophy (1985, p. 3), "experience tells us … that while statutes might not differentiate or discriminate between women and men, legal practice certainly does. Experience also tells us that the idea of a complete legal equality and even equal treatment is not a sufficient goal for feminists where, structurally, women are in a disadvantaged place vis-à-vis men." Seeing women as "objects," "others," and "things" is the consequence of a process of socialization that promotes viewing women as inferior and subordinate (Schur 1984, p. 240). The situation gets even worse for criminal women, and we may not be far away the truth if we referred them as living a "bare life" or being considered as "human waste." If prison is an unknown known in Iran, then women in Iranian prison are an even a lesser known known. This book probably would not have done justice to this subject without investigating the multiple burdens placed on the shoulders of incarcerated women in Iran: the responsibility for children, legal pressures, and cultural pressures in addition to their life in incarceration as such.

[8] For example, in Article 630, "When a man sees his wife committing Zina with another man, provided that he is certain that his wife is willing [to have sex], he can kill both of them in the same position; however if he knows that his wife acts under coercion, he may only kill the man [i.e. her rapist]. The same rule applies to assault and battery." Additionally, according to Article 1108 of Iran's Civil Code, "If the woman refuses to fulfil the duties of a wife without legitimate excuse, she will not be entitled to the cost of maintenance. It means a woman is obliged to fulfill the sexual needs of her husband at all times. This is known as the requirement of [submission], a woman's refusal to engage in sexual activity with her husband constitutes [disobedience] and can disqualify her for maintenance rights." Furthermore, according to Article 1117, "a husband can prevent his wife from occupations or technical work which are incompatible with the family interests or the dignity of himself or his wife." There is no similar exclusionary clause for women. Foucault (1980) described how power was historically exercised as a means of deducting or subtracting life, goods, services, taxes, and wealth. The above cited articles clearly suggest that men possess in Iran the privileges that are similar to the right of death and life of the sovereign in ancient times. According to Foucault's theory, "the sovereign exercised his right of life only by exercising his right to kill, he evidenced his power over life only through the death he was capable of requiring" (Foucault, 1980, p. 136).

References

Abrahamian, E. (1999). *Tortured Confessions: Prisons and Public Recantations in Modern Iran*. California: University of California Press.

Calabrese, J. (2007). Iran's War on Drugs: Holding the Line. *The Middle East Institute, Policy Brief, 3*, 1–18.

Carlsen, R. W. (1982). *The Imam and His Islamic Revolution: A Journey into Heaven and Hell.* Victoria: Snow Man Press.

Codd, H. (1998). Prisoners' Families: The "Forgotten Victims". *Probation Journal, 45*, 148–154.

Foucault, M. (1979). *Discipline and Punish: The Birth of the Prison.* New York: Vintage.

Foucault, M. (1980). The History of Sexuality. Volume One: An Introduction.

Gallahue, P., & Lines, R. (2015). The Death Penalty for Drug Offenses: Global Overview: The Extreme Fringe of Global Drug Policy.

Ghiabi, M. (2015). Drugs and Revolution in Iran: Islamic Devotion, Revolutionary Zeal and Republican Means. *Iranian Studies, 48*(2), 139–163.

Hlinomaz, O., Sheeran, S., & Bevilacqua, C. (2014). The Death Penalty for Drug Crimes in Iran: Analysis of Iran's International Human Rights Obligations. Legal Research Series, University of Essex, 9.

Iran Human Rights (IHR) and ECPM (Together Against The Death Penalty). (2016). Annual Report on the Death Penalty in Iran.

Iran Human Rights Documentation Center (IHRDC). (2015). Rights Disregarded: Prisons in the Islamic Republic of Iran.

Katouzian, H. (2004). The Short-Term Society: A Study in the Problems of Long-Term Political and Economic Development in Iran. *Middle Eastern Studies, 40*(1), 1–22.

Lösel, F., Pugh, G., Markson, L., Souza, K., & Lanskey, C. (2012). *Risk and Protective Factors in the Resettlement of Imprisoned Fathers with their Families.* Milton: Ormiston Children And Families Trust.

Macbride, R. L. (2008). Incarcerated Mothers in Cuenca, Ecuador: Perceptions of Their Environment and the Impact It Has on the Lives of Their Young Children and Their Education. Phd Dissertation, University of North Texas.

Malloch, M. (2000). *Women, Drugs and Custody: The Experiences of Women Drug Users in Prison*. Winchester: Waterside Press.

Martynowicz, A. (2011). Children of Imprisoned Parents. Danish Institute for Human Rights.

Moallem, M. (2005). *Between Warrior Brother and Veiled Sister: Islamic Fundamentalism and the Politics of Patriarchy in Iran*. Berkeley: University of California Press.

Nissaramanesh, B., Trace, M., & Roberts, M. (2005). The Rise of Harm Reduction in the Islamic Republic of Iran. Beckley Foundation Drug Policy Programme, Briefing Paper, 8.

Petersilia, J. (2005). *From Cell to Society: Who Is Returning Home?* Cambridge: Cambridge University Press.

Rejali, D. M. (1994). *Torture and Modernity: Self, Society, and State in Modern Iran*. Boulder: Westview.

Robertson, O. (2007). *The Impact of Parental Imprisonment on Children*. Geneva: Quaker United Nations Office.

Schur, E. M. (1984). *Labeling Women Deviant: Gender, Stigma, and Social Control* (p. 221). New York: Random House.

Shayestehkhou, S., Moshtagh Bidokhti, N., Eftekhar, M., & Mehrabi, F. (2008). Family Environment of Homosexual and Transsexuals in Iran. *Sexologies, 17*, S55–S56.

Smart, C., & Brophy, J. (Eds.). (1985). *Women-In-Law: Explorations in Law, Family, and Sexuality*. London: Routledge & Kegan Paul.

2

History of Prison

The First Spark of Juridical Reform in Iran

Like pre-modern Europe, Iran did not have proper prisons for holding long-term criminals, as it only had small jails for those awaiting corporal punishment, and all punishments were physical in nature. In the nineteenth century, Iran did not punish criminals through long incarceration as a matter of policy or regulation; rather, it used physical torture and violent executions. Criminals were hanged, buried alive, flogged, decapitated, disemboweled, crucified, and so on. Various actors such as the Shah, clerics, families, and communities played a role in administrating justice in Iran. As Enayat (2013, p. 29) put it, "Iran was characterized by legal pluralism."

All punishments were prescribed through the interplay between two parallel types of adjudication: the *sharia* and the *urf*. On one side was the central or provincial governments that supervised the *urf* court, which was mostly related to crimes against the *dawlat* (state) or the security of the realm such as refusing to pay taxes, causing disorder, plotting with enemies, and four specific crimes: theft, murder, rape, and assault. *urf* courts were not based on fixed regulations and procedures, as

N. R. Anaraki, *Prison in Iran*, Palgrave Studies in Prisons and Penology,
https://doi.org/10.1007/978-3-030-57169-6_2

decisions were made on the basis of unwritten traditions or arbitrarily. As Malcom observed, "this law, if it can be termed as such, is never written" (quoted in Enayat 2013, p. 33). Criminals were punished by the governor based on *maslahat* (their own discretion). High authorities and governors were in charge of imposing penalties for serious crimes, while petty crimes were dealt with by the village head or sheriff. However, the Shah was the highest authority in *urf* jurisdiction who took charge of prosecutions for the four specific crimes, particularly murder. As a matter of fact, in cases of murder, both *urf* and *sharia* were involved, since murder was governed by the *sharia* law of retaliation or *qisas* and also permitted by the Shah. On the other side were clerics, who oversaw the *sharia* courts and enforced religious laws to deal with four categories of crimes: *Hudud* (punishments specific to the *sharia* law), *qisas* (retaliatory punishments), *Deyat* (blood money), and *Tazirat* (deterrent punishments) (The four categories of crimes will be explained in detail in the section related to the Islamic Revolution penal code in 1979). As Werner (2000) argued, we have to be very cautious when discussing the concept of courts since there were no formal structures or organizations in place. The boundary between *sharia* and *urf* was unclear and vague since they have not applied totally different types of law. According to Enayat (2013), a combination of religious and customary laws was practiced by both branches of legal authorities. However, as Amanat (2009, p. 185) states, "neither the jurists nor the state attempted to define the spheres of *shar* and *orf* or to demarcate their boundaries through codification, let alone breach the informal boundaries between them."

It is well documented that Iran was reformed, militarily and economically in particular, several times before the Constitutional Revolution during the Qajar monarchy (1905–1909). The first spark of juridical reform in Iran was initiated during the last years of Nasser id-Din Shah Qajar (1848–1896), who ruled over the country for almost half a century. Juridical transitions were affected by the reformers' protests against the traditional judicial system. These protesters were known as the "*munavar al-fekr*" and "*rushan fekran*" (both literally mean "enlightened thinkers") who questioned the lack of consistency and distinction between *urf* and *sharia*, the prevalence of judicial torture and corporal punishments, the excessive power of the clergy, and so on (Abrahamian 1999,

p. 23). There were three attempts to reform legal institutions, and almost all of them did not have long-lasting effects. Although Qajar kings were not interested in sharing their absolute and totalitarian power, the first attempt at legal reform was made by Qajar reformers such as Amir Kabir, a Nasser id-Din Shah's prime minister, who changed the name of the central divan (a judicial institution) to Divan-e Bozorg-e Padeshahi (the High Court of the Sovereign) to unify and centralize the legal system, established *divankhane* (House of Justice) in the provinces, and banned harsh physical punishments (Enayat 2013). Additionally, in 1851, officials or *divanbegi* were introduced to supervise the cases that were brought to the local *urf* and *sharia* courts in the provinces, to refer serious cases to the central *Divankhaneh* in Tehran, and to report on the quality of justice in those courts to *Divankhneh-ye Adlieh-ye Azam* (Grand Justice Ministry) (Bakhash 1978, p. 84). Furthermore, in 1870, the provincial governors' authority was limited in order to issue a unified legal structure for the *urf* courts, which would allow to apply legal decisions and judgments in all criminal matters (Adamiyat and Nāteq 1977, pp. 178–179). Although it has been claimed that the Qajar reforms aimed at centralizing, rationalizing, and unifying the administrative and legal system did not last long, significant juridical changes over the course of the nineteenth century were tangible through the Shah's assassination attempts.

The first attempt to assassinate Nasser id-Din Shah in 1852 failed and Babis (the assailant) was stoned to death. However, the Shah died from a second assassination attempt in 1896, Kirmani (the assailant) was incarcerated and then executed, in contrast to Babis's execution in 1852. Additionally, some drastic juridical changes such as decreasing the rate of public executions and the vanishing of penal processions occurred gradually from 1885 to 1896. Judicial and prison reforms during the Qajar monarchy stemmed from increasing familiarity with the western judicial system, which guided reformers toward improving the legal and prison system. Also, Nasser id-Din Shah was one of the first Persian monarchs who officially visited Europe, and one of his goals was to collect "all information and gathering experiences, which can be valuable for the Persian government and nation" (Motadel 2011, p. 193). As Curzon said (1966, p. 457), "fortunately, the visits of the Shah to Europe, and the increasing influence of civilized opinion, have had a wonderful effect in mitigating the barbarity of this truly merciless and oriental code, and cases of unnecessary torture are now rarely heard of."

Prisons in the Qajar Reign

There were two types of prisons in the Qajar reign: governmental prisons and private prisons. Governmental prisons were divided into two groups: *Daro-al-hokome*, which were designed to keep prisoners in cities and governed by the Shah or Shah's deputies; and *Siyahchal* (dungeons), which kept political prisoners as far as possible from the cities. Private prisons were considered temporary detention centers, usually the private homes of representatives of the state such as regents and sheriffs, used to hold criminals for a short time prior to disposition by *urf* or *sharia* (Abbasi 2012). In religious events (e.g. *Ashora*[1]), prisoners were provided with a *Nazr* (a vow or commitment to carry out an act in Islam), usually food or clothes. In the Qajar reign, prisoners' clothes were provided by their families and the relatives of inmates, and most inmates survived with just one set of clothes during their incarceration (Majdoleslam kermani 1971). Since prison walls were not high enough and there was a shortage of guards, 10 or 14 prisoners were chained together in group by a *Kand* (a big piece of wood that held their legs) or *Khalili* (a kind of chain that held their legs). According to Nazem al-Eslam, prisons under Nasser id-Din Shah Qajar's reign were dark, wet, stinking, and dirty, and contained nothing but chains, shackles, fleas, and lice. On special occasions, prisoners were provided with five small pieces of bread daily with almost no water.

Prisoners had restricted communications with the outside world; however, guards, for either humanitarian or financial purposes, smuggled paper and pens into the prisons and mailed prisoners' letters or asked recently released prisoners to do so. Those inmates who were wealthier or had a higher status in the society spent their sentences in more

[1] "Ashura is the tenth day of Muharram, the first month in the Islamic Calendar. It marks the day that Husayn ibn Ali, the grandson of the Islamic prophet Muhammad, was martyred in the Battle of Karbala. Ashura is a major holiday and occasion for pilgrimage in Shia Islam, as well as a recommended but non-obligatory day of fasting in Sunni Islam" https://en.wikipedia.org/wiki/Ashura.

comfortable circumstances than others. High-status criminals were not chained, had *Nokar* (servants), were provided with high-quality foods, and were treated well by guards; however, guards or even administrators expected bribes from high-status criminals in return for the provided services (Sayah Mahalati 1988). Interrogation along with torture were common in the Qajar prisons, and while no precise information is available about tortures for different crimes, some tortures used were *Tange-ghajar* (placing small pieces of wood between the fingers and tightening and pushing them) (Shaghaghi 1974); *Eshkelak* (placing wood or iron pieces between the fingers and pressing them) (Mokhtari 1950); *Dagh-o-Derafsh* (burning the body with hot irons) (Majdoleslam Kermani 1971); sexual harassment of criminals' children (Tajolsaltane 1982); and rubbing oil on criminals' children's legs and burning them (Kasravi 2004). This suggests that the inclusion of the prisoners' children into the penal system has historical precedents (I will return to this issue in Chap. 4. Since none of the prisons in the Qajar reign were designed to be used as prisons, criminals could not be kept there for long. All prisons were dark, humid, and without adequate ventilation; however, as discussed earlier, the social status of criminals brought prosperity to them, even in harsh circumstances. While other prisoners did not have food to survive, they had their own cooks or could even order food from outside and smoke Hookahs with the guards. Due to this, intellectuals and reformers questioned the juridical system and prison conditions.

The Constitutional Revolution

The juridical system was shaken drastically from 1905 to 1909 by the Constitutional Revolution, when constitutionalists initiated reforms that led to changes in the practices of government, law, and administration. The Constitutional Revolution was "incomparably longer and deeper than any other Middle Eastern revolution of the period" (Enayat 2005, p. 166). As Shirali (2017, p. 2) states, "the Constitutional Revolution opened a new page in Iran's history." The first criminal law legislation in the Iranian legal system was passed by the first parliament in 1911;

however, it was replaced by the General Penal Code in 1925 after the transition of the monarchy from Qajar to Pahlavi (Tavana 2014).

After 1909, *urf* was changed to *Adliyeh* (Justice Ministry), and a specific office was established to decide which cases would go to the *sharia* courts (Abrahamian 1999). In fact, one of the most important demands of reformers during the Iranian Constitutional Revolution was to establish *Adliyeh* or *edalat-khaneh* (House of Justice or Justice Ministry). "House of justice meant a system of state courts that would function on the basis of Iran's law, not on the arbitrary whim of the monarch or the prince-governors of Iran's far-flung provinces" (Enayat 2013, p. 1). By establishing *Adliyeh*, cities' rulers were not allowed to punish, torture, or execute criminals; rather, they were supposed to transfer them to the *Adliyeh* in Tehran. In other words, the *Adliyeh* was put in charge of investigating and prosecuting crimes. Additionally, reformers established a clear line between the state and citizens by determining precise punishments for different types of crimes. The modifications to the legal system of the country officially made a distinction between *sharia* and *urf*, which paved the way to further recognition of the influence of religious elements in the legal system. Clerics had control over family law, laws of marriage and divorce, or, in other words, the clergy "continued to exercise de facto jurisdiction in most areas of civil law" (Nader Entessar 1988, p. 98). Also, juridical torture was banned, executions were restricted to hanging or firing squads, a national gendarmerie (police force) was organized, and, eventually, a Tehran Central Prison or *Zendan-e Markazi* as a temporary detention center was established with the help of a Swedish officer. In the Tehran Central Prison, according to the reformer prisoners, adequate ventilation and light in the new prisons were considered important objectives. Additionally, solitary areas were designed as part of the new prisons to hold murderers.

However, before establishing the central prison, there were prison number one and number two, which were located exactly in front of each other, with large walls, damp and dark conditions, blood on the walls, and washrooms in the cells. Number one prison was known as a "dark prison" or *Siah Chal* (dark hole), and the second one was lighter than the first. Going to the former was known as being "buried alive" and was even used as a torture for political prisoners since murderers and thieves were kept there. Prisoners were kept in cells with no beds, fresh air, or light. Lice were everywhere. Prison number two was originally designed to keep prisoners just for 15 days, as inmates would go blind or become handicapped if they were kept there longer (Eftekhari 1991, p. 44). Prisoners in prison number two could walk in the yard for a couple of minutes every day; however, they could not talk together. In the summer, the walls were so hot that the guards would make fun of the prisoners during their walking time. The guards told each other "lets take them to heaven." Prisoners had one cup of tea with one sugar cube for breakfast and a piece of bread and *Ash* for lunch and dinner. As Avanessian (1979, pp. 8–9) states, "even a dog could not eat them." Prison conditions were even worse in other provinces. As one of the prisoners described, Bandar Abbas prison was known as the "hell of Iran" since it was so hot. It was a muddy building with 40 to 60 prisoners, food was dates for 16 months, and prisoners ate dates instead of eating sugar cubes, fruits, and meat. In the winter, prisoners usually drink the rainwater, which was unhealthy. Prisoners preferred to drink the salty water meant for washing hands. They were in a cell with three other prisoners who rarely talked since they had different opinions regarding political issues. There was no shower in the prison, prisoners were transferred to the city to take shower. All prisoners in Kermanshah prison were kept in one deep, fetid, dirty enclosure, which was about 156 meters with no equipment. Poor prisoners in Mashahad starved and a significant number of them died as a result of a lack of cleanliness and hygiene (Hosseini 1991, pp. 44–45). According to Avanessian (1979, p. 22), the prison of Tabriz was full of *Dehghan* (farmers) who had fights with landowners. Political prisoners made many efforts to communicate with them; however, there was no success since the guards watched them all the time. In other words, not only was political prisoners' intra-communication restricted, but also their communication with other political prisoners. Since the warden and guards were well aware that political prisoners intended to educate common criminals about daily political issues around the world, the fear of enlightening the prisoners made guards cautious about communications among prisoners (Fig. 2.1).

Likewise, during the nineteenth-century reforms, the Constitutional Revolution, despite many contradictions and ambivalences, found its

Fig. 2.1 Map of Iran

own path to altering the functions of the state, law, and justice in Iran by establishing an independent law-making department that was separate from the Shah and clerics' will, engaged in the writing and enforcement of regulations, and introduced European-inspired legal procedures (Enayat 2013, pp. 79–80). Since administration of the criminal justice in the nineteenth century was unstructured, unwritten, despotic, and arbitrary, in some cases, based on the written Islamic law with the ultimate supervision of the Shah, issuing the penal code in 1915 was not easy. Opposition, rejections, and objections mostly came from the sharia courts or *ulama* (clerics). For instance, Shaykh Asadollah declared, "our country already has a criminal law and that is the law of the *sharia*, and the minister of justice must bring no other bill to the *Majles*. All that can be envisaged is the codification of the laws that exist in the sharia. They must be organized and codified and then enforced" (quoted in Enayat 2013, p. 106). However, a minister of justice, Forughi, stated, "it is very clear to those who have been insiders in the Ministry of Justice that more of the complaints of the past years, which people think are to do with individuals, in fact go back to the absence of laws. In truth, running a judiciary without laws is a bizarre thing. There may be good will, we may have the law of sharia and people in the Adlieh who are learned in sharia affairs and can do their work, but there is still an urgent need for law" (quoted in Enayat 2013, pp. 106–107). Finally, in 1917, a draft of Islamic law was reviewed, a modern Penal Code based on the French penal code was published, and the Special Criminal Court was established in Tehran. The modern Penal Code includes no corporal punishment. However, the struggle between *urf* in the *Adliye* courts and *sharia* in the Special Criminal Court became even more tangible in the modern penal code. According to Article 348 of the Penal Code, "Penalties are set out in this law for public order. Likewise, felonies that are discovered and investigated in accordance with the principles of Islam and whose consequences are multiple and defined are in jurisdiction of the Special Criminal Court, and after legal trial and the verdict of the presiding *sharia* judge, will be punished in accordance with the *Hodud* and *Tazirat* as laid down in the *sharia*" (Enayat 2013, p. 108).

A Root-and-Branch Revamping of the Whole Judicial System

Real judicial reform did not occur until 1925 when Reza Shah, the founder of the Pahlavi dynasty, was chosen as a ruler of Iran by parliament. Reza Shah's first act was to overhaul the traditional legal system by reforming the Penal Code by separating it from the Islamic roots and moving it toward a European legal tradition, and particularly inspired by France and Belgium, with the help of Ali Akbar Dadvar, a justice minister who was educated at a European university. Efforts toward the secularization, centralization, and modernization of the criminal justice system eventually occurred in Iran by the time when the Penal Code was presented in Parliament in February 1926. The new reformers realized that corporal punishments and religious discrimination could not be eliminated "without a root-and-branch revamping of the whole judicial system" (Abrahamian 1999, p. 25). However, due to a lack of trained personnel and to avoid social tension, Ali Akbar Dadvar did not totally reject the cooperation of clerics who had previously served in the *Adliye*, despite having the authority to limit the jurisdiction of *sharia* courts (Enayat 2013, p. 146).

Besides the efforts made to effectively secularize the justice system, there were still some references to the Islamic principles in the 1925 penal code, particularly Article 1, which clearly declared that "all prescribed punishments are for the preservation of public order in the country and will be supervised by the *Adliye* courts (court of justice). Additionally, those crimes that are discovered and investigated based on the Islamic laws will be punished according to the *Huddud* and *Tazirat* laid down in the sharia." Furthermore, in the 1926 version of the Penal Code, corporal punishment was admitted in cases involving children to perhaps protect them from the consequences of incarceration. Besides, the footprints of patriarchal customary law were traceable.

In spite of the clergy's concerns regarding the future of administrating punishments based on *sharia* laws and Parliament's promises on the continued functioning of the *sharia* courts, sharia justice and courts gradually vanished and closed. Since there was no room for *sharia* punishments, there was a title with no functions, particularly after a 1973 amendment, when *sharia* courts were abolished and the application of Islamic law altogether was formally removed from the Iranian legal system (Rahami 2005, p. 586). After the elimination of *sharia* courts, courts on the national, regional, and provincial levels were established, and all lawyers and judges were required to have a university degree either from a Tehran law school or a Western university. Corporal punishments and public executions gradually diminished to protect society as part of the framework of humanitarianism. Prison conditions were improved, and many prisons with modern facilities were established. Emphasis was put on separating prisoners based on their crimes and ages and also on providing them with more tolerable conditions (i.e. fresh air, light, yards to exercise in, and mental relaxation). Recidivists and professional criminals were kept in a separate section from other offenders and offenders between 15 and 18 were kept apart from adults. Additionally, rehabilitation to prepare prisoners for post-incarceration played a significant role in the reforming program. Prisoners were provided with a wide variety of handicraft and mechanical training to survive post-release life. The rapid process of establishing prisons nationwide was initiated due to a lack of prisons and the poor conditions of prisons in Iran (Hosseini 1991, p. 46). The capacity of Mashhad prison was 200 prisoners, yet 900 prisoners were kept there (Hosseini 1991, p. 44). The Tehran Central prison, which was designed for 400 prisoners, housed 1000 by the end of 1920 (Pishevari 1944, p. 147). A former prisoner wrote that, one day, 500 Kurd political prisoners were sent to the Central prison. They were forced to take off their national clothes, shave their hair, and put on prisoners' clothes. As a result of overcrowding, they did not have individual trials, and all of them were given the same sentence. Most of them died in the prison as a result of malnutrition, as they were only given a small amount of yogurt daily. They did not have contact with their family members either (Avanessian 1979, pp. 61–62). As a result of a shift in attention toward prolonged incarceration as a replacement for corporal punishment, an increasing number of political prisoners in the aftermath of the 1917 Revolution in Russia, and poor prison conditions, a large number of prisons were established during Reza Shah's reign in 34 cities including Tehran, Semnan, Khoy, Malayer, Tabriz, Ardebil, Ghazvin, Khozestan, Kerman, Kermanshah, Rasht, Shiraz, Qom, Sari, Damghan, Khorasan, and Nahavand, which put a heavy burden on prison facilities. However, most of those prisons were built later, in the 1950s–1960s (Abrahamian 1999, p. 27).

One of the most important prisons that was built in 1920 and opened in 1929 was Qasr prison in Tehran. As Abrahamian (1999, p. 27) states, "Qasr become a notorious symbol of the Pahlavi state and the new judicial system." It had 14 yards and different sections to separate inmates based on their crime committed and age. The Qasr building had nine blocks. Short-term inmates were kept in major block number one; the most dangerous criminals were kept in blocks 5 and 6, which were messy and dirty; privileged prisoners and former officials were kept in block 8; and political prisoners were kept in the clean and ventilated block 7, in which they had their own clothes and beddings. The high, thick, barbed wired walls, which were protected by armed guards, not only hid the occasional execution from public view, but also separated prisoners from the rest of society. As Abrahamian (1999, p. 27) states, Qasr was called "*Faramoshkhane* (house of forgetfulness): the outside world was supposed to forget its inmates; its inmates were supposed to forget the outside world." Also, the most intolerable and inhuman features of prisons such as solitary cells and absolute silence were more or less eliminated. In the first days of Qasr's opening, when it was not yet overcrowded, every two prisoners were kept in one cell, and they were guarded in the yard. However, due to the increasing number of inmates and a lack of medicine, typhus epidemics spread, and many prisoners died (Eftekhari 1991).

As a result of growing political activities, especially by communists, the rate of incarceration suddenly increased. From 1929 to 1930, Qasr had 300 prisoners, 18 of whom were political prisoners. By 1940, about 2000 prisoners were incarcerated, 200 of whom were political prisoners. Although most of these prisoners were not physically tortured since it was not permitted, solitary confinement was used as the most common torture for prisoners. Physical force was normally used in the Qasr prison only on common criminals (e.g. spies and burglars). However, it is well documented that flogging and whipping were not only used on common criminals but also on political prisoners. The Qasr warden later declared that the flogging of political prisoners was not for extracting information but meant to force them to obey the prison rules. However, four associates of Reza Shah, including the Qasr warden, were eventually accused of murdering prisoners (Abrahamian 1999). Thieves and embezzlers possessed the highest status in Qasr prison, as they were allowed family visitations on their own convenient time; they could leave the prison for a couple of hours in return for paying bribes to guards; they ordered *Shahaneh* (luxury) foods; they filled their cells with comfortable couches and beds; and they smuggled opium, alcohol, and cigarettes into the prison (Pishevari 1944).

According to Alavi, another torture for inmates was being incarcerated with a lot of people; "you are hemmed in, surrounded by people you have nothing in common with, and you are forced to eat with them, talk with them, sleep with them. How long can you go on talking to someone about personal matters?... Or when you are trying to think or have a daydream, someone comes along with a dirty story, gesturing grossly, and you are finding yourself listening" (Raffat 1985, p. 132). Another torture for prisoners in Qasr, for political prisoners in particular, was being incarcerated for years without being sentenced. As stated by Alavi, they were in an "utterly dehumanized limbo" or "up to the air" in comparison with other criminals (e.g. murderers and thieves).

In 1938, drugs as well as books and pens were smuggled into the prison. Prisoners in Qasr created various activities to keep their minds busy and break the monotony. Reading books, especially after 1938, when Reza Shah ordered that prisoners could have non-political books, was one of the forms of entertainment in the prison. While some books, especially political ones, were not permitted in the prison, books were smuggled regularly to the extent that guards were likely aware of this but preferred to close their eyes to keep prisoners busy with reading and not protesting. According to Alavi, "two people crammed into one cell, every day hearing the same words, this for me was unbearable. Well, a book, of course, gave a person a little comfort; it exercised one's mind" (Raffat 1985, p. 51). In spite of this, there were spies who informed guards regarding the existence of pens and books, especially in political prisoners' cells, since possessing any writing materials was considered a serious offense. According to a former prisoner in Qasr, prison was like a school (Raffat 1985) or a lively university (Ovanessian 1944) in which prisoners learnt various languages (e.g. English, Russian, and French); however, one of the most important influences on prisoners was to become politicized whether one liked it or not, since, as Abrahamian (1999, p. 28) states, Qasr prison "obtained the reputation of being the regime's political prison, and it retained this reputation until the 1970s." Another form of entertainment was exercising and playing volleyball in the prison yards, which encouraged even "opium-smoking guards" to join with the prisoners (Raffat 1985, p. 50). Team-working was not the case during educational classes or physical activities, but prisoners collectively saved each other's lives during a typhus epidemic in the prison. However, the only available entertainment in some prisons in 1941, such as Filiyeh in

Khozestan, was a small chamber with a tiny hole to transfer bread and water to the prison (Kasravi 1942).

The rate of incarceration in 1935 was still not high in comparison with the rate in 1978 and during the Islamic Republic. The incarceration rate in 1935 was 2.7 to 6.2 prisoners per 100,000 members of the population, while in 1978, before the Islamic Revolution, it was 25 per 100,000 members of the population (Enayat 2013; Madani 2006). In 1935, the number of imprisonments was as follows: (a) offences sentenced by ordinary courts: 2200; (b) offences sentenced by military courts: 1072; (c) temporary prisoners arrested under the order of ordinary courts: 1873; (d) temporary prisoners arrested under the order of the military courts: 416; (e) Tehran political prisoners: 104; (f) political prisoners in other provinces: 5; (g) criminal migrants in Tehran: 474; (h) criminals from other provinces: 1700; (i) migrants arrested after attempting to escape: 18; (j) prisoners from tribes in Tehran: 160; and (k) prisoners from tribes in the provinces: 40 (Hosseini 1991, pp. 44–45).

Interregnum (1941–1953)

Royal autocracy and the rule of Reza Shah Pahlavi ended in 1941 and re-emerged in 1953 when Mohammad Reza Shah, with the assistance of allies, that is, Britain and America took full control over the military. The period between 1941 and 1953 was considered as an interregnum by Iranians. Two salient phenomena during these 13 years remarkably affected the society: Dr. Mohammad Mossadeq and *Hezb-e-Tudeh-e* Iran (the party of the Iranian Masses) or the *Tudeh* party (Abrahamian 1999). Mossadeq was the 35th prime minister of Iran from 1951 to 1953 and is well-known for criticizing the royal family because of the tremendous involvement and control of foreign actors over the country, limiting the Monarchy's powers, nationalizing Iran's oil industry, and calling Britain, which was the majority shareholder of Iranian oil from 1941, an enemy. Also, he called the *Majles* (the Iranian parliament) a "den of thieves." As a result of anti-foreigner policies, especially returning the whole control of oil to the Iranian government, allies, that is, the United States and United Kingdom protested against Mossadeq, and Iran witnessed serious political and economic crises, which significantly decreased Mossadeq's popularity and political power. The coup of August 19, 1953, in favor of strengthening the rule of Mohammad Reza Shah and overthrowing the prime minister was initiated by *Tudeh* party members under the influence of the United States and United Kingdom. Following the 1953 coup, almost all the prime minister's associates were imprisoned, tortured, and executed.

As Abrahamian (1999, p. 80) states, the *Tudeh* party, which was founded in 1941, was "initially a hybrid of socialism and communism, parliamentary liberalism and revolutionary radicalism, Marxism from Western and Leninism from the Bolshevik Revolution" and managed to be the first Iranian mass organization with 2200 members in 1945. After the coup, the process of arresting and torturing *Tudeh* activists was started initially by the *Rokn-e Dovom* (Second Bureau), which monitored civilians, and followed by the secret intelligence service, SAVAK, which was established in 1957 by Mohammad Reza Shah. Prisoners were tortured to obtain information about the *Tudeh* organization, other members, safe houses for their gatherings, and so on. According to one *Tudeh* leader, the torture in the prisons after 1953 included "barbaric practices" (Ansari 1996, p. 416). SAVAK applied various types of methods to extract information, from whipping and breaking hands to suspending prisoners on hooks (Abrahamian 1999; Ansari 1996). According to Abrahamian, torture was considered as a practice of the old Qajar days or fascists in Europe. As one of the political activists stated, it was not "in our calculation that we were going to deal with fascism" (Baqeyi 1994, p. 446).

After the coup, the most famous prisons in Tehran, such as Qasr and the Central prison, along with the provincial prisons were overcrowded. It is documented that even prisons such as *Falak al-falak* in Khorramabad, which was small, local, and considered a caravanserai,[2] became a political prison with 500 political prisoners (Maleki 1956; Lotfi 2013). About 117 of the political prisoners in 1953 were sent to *Khark* prison in Bushehr, which was not just a prison but provided an opportunity for the state to treat prisoners arbitrarily. "We were not provided with enough food, and once we protested, they even decreased our food share. We usually bought salt, flour, and meat to survive" (Rahnama 2013). According

[2] A place where travelers could stop and have a rest.

to Keshavarz (1984), prisoners in the *Khark* prison created a large *komun*[3] to manage their finances. They also had several collective activities from cooking, grocery, cleaning, washing clothes, and collecting rainwater to drink, to swimming, singing, celebrating (e.g. Nowruz, Constitutional Day, and January 1), playing games (e.g. volleyball and chess), and learning languages (e.g. Persian, Azari, English, French, and Russian). On special occasion, fruits could be bought from local smugglers and ships. Additionally, *Khark* prisoners created social circles—various groups of intellectuals—from opponents and proponents of Mossadeq to the "simple folk." According to Keshavarz, dealing with humidity, heat, infection, and a lack of medicine in *Khark* were disastrous during the summer. However, some prisoners were transferred from Khark to Borazjan prison, where the low monthly rations they received were barely enough to buy food, especially in conditions in which necessities should be bought from Shiraz (133 km far from Borazjan) since there were no shopping stores in Borazjan. Almost all money was spent on buying ice to deal with the near 50°C days in Borazjan (Haghi 1993). The condition in the Qasr prison was not better; for instance, prisoners in section two were the poorest inmates and could not afford to buy life necessities. According to Khameyi (1993, pp. 178–179), "if there was no financial assistance given to prisoners in section seven to buy tea, clothes, cigarettes, etc. we could not survive. While food was not an issue in section seven, it was one of the most important reasons behind the protests and chaos in section two. Also, some sections had charcoal ovens to cook rice, egg, beans, and meat, but these were banned in section two, so we made a stove out of cans and charcoal. Once the guards found out how we cooked food, they banned the distribution of cans in our section. Section seven had facilities for reading and writing, while having a pen or one piece of paper was a crime in section two."

After a 1953 coup, about 31 *Tudeh* members were executed, 144 got life sentences, 119 got 15 years of incarceration, and 79 activists were sentenced to 10 years of imprisonment (Abrahamian 1999, pp. 92–93). Although "the regime became increasingly brutal from the early 1960s

[3] Large proportion of prisoners organized into informal groups based on the same interests, especially political preferences and convictions.

on" (Enayat 2013, p. 181), it "preferred that the public forget the immediate past as soon as possible" (Abrahamian 1999, p. 98). As a result, Mossadeq and most *Tudeh* prisoners were released after four years. Afterward, prisons such as *Khark* and *Falak al-falak* were closed immediately. Needless to say, *Tudeh* military officers were required to sign conventional letters of regret to be released, and most of them were convinced to do so after being persuaded by the *Tudeh*'s leaders (Amoui 1993). Therefore, the number of *Tudeh* prisoners decreased to 24 by the late 1960s. However, the conditions of prisons did not change dramatically compared to the past, but prisoners were provided with radios, TVs, reading rooms, and indoor gyms (Abrahamian 1999).

Prison Life from 1971 to 1977

On February 8, 1971, in the *Siahkal* incident, 13 young, anti-regime Marxists attacked a police station at the village of *Siahkal* near the Caspian Sea and killed two gendarmes. The guerrillas were arrested by the police and executed; however, this incident became a model for other groups to use to challenge the authority of the regime and specifically the first person of the country, the shah. Marxist *Fedayi* (Self-Sacrificers), for instance, concluded that their "immediate task is to form small cells and launch assaults on the enemy to destroy the repressive 'atmosphere' and to prove to the masses that armed struggle is the only way to liberation" (Abrahamian 1982, p. 485). Meanwhile, the regime used a wide range of tactics to isolate and hunt down the guerrillas. First, they accused them of being atheists and terrorists through the Shah's propaganda machine (Daneshvar 2016). Then, during the period from 1971 to 1977, 197 guerrillas were killed in armed struggle, 93 were executed, 45 died under torture, and 33 committed suicide before being arrested. It is well documented that most guerrillas were members of the intelligentsia, under 35 years old, and affiliated with three different organizations: Marxist Fedayi (Self-Sacrificers), Muslim Mojahedin (Holy Warriors), and Marxists Mojahedin. Once again, a drastic rate of incarceration, brutality, and torture became measures used to deal with social issues in Iran. The state won all its battles against guerrillas by recruiting 5000 new employees and informants to SAVAK and providing them with "scientific" methods of torturing, creating a *Komiteh* (committee) located in the central jail in Tehran for interrogations, building maximum security prisons in the provinces, and adding women's blocks in Qasr (Abrahamian 1999). Prisons such as Evin, which was built in 1971, with a capacity of 320 prisoners was expanded to the extent that by 1977, 1500 prisoners could be imprisoned. As Hamidian (2010, p. 145) states, "the political sections of Qasr prison, from 1971 to 1972, had never been that crowded before, and there was no space for sleeping. All the corridors were full of prisoners."

As a result of this overcrowding, some of the prisoners in Qasr were transferred to *Adel Abad* prison in Shiraz and *Vakil Abad* prison in Mashhad. *Vakil Abad* was one of the newest prisons, with 4 three-story buildings, bathrooms with hot water and washrooms in each cell, clinics and dental buildings, a relatively large sock knitting workshop, and three-story beds for 12 prisoners in each block. Approximately 90% of the "ordinary prisoners"[4] in *Vakil Abad* were poor, from rural areas, sold cigarettes, and worked in the factories. Political prisoners and other criminals were kept in the same blocks in Vakil Abad. One of the most important features of Vakil Abad that distinguished it from the other prisons was the visiting rooms. Prisoners in *Qasr* had family visits behind two rows of iron, were about two meters away from their visitor, with a wired net on each side for surveillance and control and one guard in between to overhear dialogue. While in *Vakil Abad*, prisoners sat behind thick glass, talked by phone with visitors, and guards had full control over their conversation, which left no room for forbidden discussions between prisoners and visitors (Hamidian 2010).

Although torture was a common part of incarceration in most periods in Iran, it became much more explicit, brutal, and sophisticated from 1971 to 1977 as a result of the systematic training of interrogators along with an official permission from the regime to apply physical and psychological pressure (e.g. "bastinado, sleep deprivation, extensive solidarity confinement, glaring search lights, standing in one place for hours on end, nail extraction, snakes (favored for use with women), electrical

[4] Non-political prisoners.

shocks with cattle prods, cigarette burns, sitting in hot grills, acid dripped into nostrils, near-drownings, mock executions, electrocution, humiliation by being raped, forced to stand naked, and threatening to rape their wives, sisters, and even mothers" or "being raped by wood or a bottle") to extract information regarding the addresses of safe houses and the next gatherings of the guerrillas (Abrahamian 1999, pp. 106–107; Tabrizi 2004, p. 120).

Evin in those days had no reading room, had no radio, was provided with censored newspapers and TV programs, and was under surveillance by hidden cameras. As Amoui (1993, p. 138) states, the new prisons such as Evin were even worse than the old ones since the privacy of prisoners was constantly breached by the guards, and there was no greenery, as "there was nothing but iron and steel." Prisoners in Evin woke up at 6:00 am, ate breakfast at 8:00 am, walked in the yard for one and a half hour, had classes at 3:00 pm, and went to sleep at 11:00 pm. Sexual relationships were a taboo, and prisoners did their best to control all possible provocations. For instance, as Abrahamian 1999, p. 109) states, "during television hours, two prisoners—usually one from the *Mojahedin* and one from the *Fedayi*—sat on each side of the television with a drape to block the view if any scantily clothed women unexpectedly appeared on the screen." In the Evin, prisoners organized their own *Komun*s, and each *Komun* had leaders and banks to manage the finances of the group. The source of money was families' gifts and money sent to the prison. One of the tortures that usually applied against political prisoners was sending them among "ordinary prisoners." On one hand, this was a threat to them since they did not have any friends, and also they were exposed to sexual assaults. According to Tabrizi (2004, p. 306), "as a result of singing revolutionary songs, they sent us among murderers and drug dealers. They had very large rooms. Although it was forbidden for both sides to communicate, "ordinary prisoners" used all opportunities to communicate and help us. For us, who lived among political prisoners with the restricted rules and policies, it was challenging to live among criminals." For instance, some members of the Fifty-Three Group (*Tudeh* Party of Iran) were transferred to section five of *Falake* prison in Tehran. In 1953, about 400 high-profile criminals (i.e. professional thieves and murderers) were kept in a 15 by 8-meter room—section five—of *Falake* or *Komite* prison with no bathroom, and they were referred to as *Gav Dani* (cattle). As Khameyi (1993, p. 127) describes, there was not enough space for everyone in this section to sleep on their back or stomach, and all had to sleep *ketabi* (on side). The guards even assigned three prisoners—*tark-e daran* (prisoners provided with a whip)—to punish those who did not obey the sleeping rule. On the other hand, this could be used as an opportunity to communicate with the ordinary people and be informed about the political news outside prison.

However, the solidarity, alliances, and integration among political prisoners drew attention very soon, which was a warning for the warden and guards. Therefore, in some prisons, for instance, *Vakil Abad*, to avoid any unexpected influences of political prisoners on other criminals, political prisoners' contact with ordinary prisoners was limited. They were not allowed to serve them food in the food court, and instead each *Komun* was provided with food in their blocks. In *Qasr* prison, as a result of the intensive solidarity among political prisoners, the guards warned prisoners that there is no "us"; there is only "me" in prison (Khameyi 1993, p. 128). In contrast to *Qasr* prison in *Vakil Abad*, there was an extensive archive of books and newspapers, a color television, large volleyball and basketball courts, and weights for physical exercises. However, all the facilities in Vakil Abad were boycotted in 1973 as a result of the political activities of prisoners inside and outside prisons (Hamidian 2010). On some occasions, political prisoners were used by drug dealers to smuggle drugs into the prison. Additionally, some non-political prisoners were educated and trained by political prisoners and changed from drug dealers to political activists after being released (Mazaheri 2005). Additionally, there was another reason for keeping political and non-political prisoners together, which was agitating political prisoners and then accusing them of being involved in riots and chaos to put pressure on them or even execute them (Haghi 1993).

In *Qasr*, the daily schedule was almost the same as in the Evin. Prisoners woke up at 6:00–6:30 am, exercised until 8:00 am, listened to the radio, played volleyball, and had the same routine. In 1970, due to prison overcrowding and a lack of space, some prisoners slept in the yard next to the volleyball field and washrooms. As Etemadzade (1991) states, some prisoners in Qasr slept in the rooms, and while all rooms had a ceiling fan—all facilities in the prison were purchased by prisoners—it was still hot and suffocating. In *Qasr* prison, both political and non-political prisoners were kept together; six prisoners were "ordinary prisoners," almost half of them were political prisoners, and the rest were Kurdish and Arab spies on the Iraq border or Azari spies on the Soviet border who were informants (*zir hashti*[5]) in the prison as well. For lunch, each *Komun* has its own food and *sofreh* (tablecloths), which sat next to next in the rooms. None of the prisoners were informed about gifts or money that were sent by families; all were considered public property in *Komun*. One of the largest *Komuns* in which 80% of prisoners were members was formed in section three of Qasr. All activities of members of the *Komun*, from eating food, cleaning rooms, washing clothes, and shopping, were organized by the *Komun*. Before Mohmmad Reza Shah's reign, as Avanessian (1979, p. 53) states, class conflict was tangible among communists, landowners, village owners, parliament lawyers, and farmers. Village owners often took the posture of the "father of the nation" and did not talk with poor prisoners, and they particularly distanced themselves from communists. Despite all restrictions, communists communicated with farmers to enlighten them regarding political issues in the country. However, in 1970, class conflicts were not a prominent feature since the elites were mostly banished abroad or to the private business sector (Abrahamian 1999).

In 1975, the number of incarcerated women in *Qasr* prison reached a peak of 200 since the regime considered any political activities such as distributing a single political statement, reading even one forbidden book, hiding a political activist even for one night, typing political statements, or participating in protests as an attempt to violate national security. Women political prisoners in *Qasr* were deprived of family visits, books, newspapers, TV, warm clothes, and underwear. They were all kept in four rooms with two rows of three-story beds; the space between the beds was no more than one meter. They were allowed to use the bathroom three times daily and in "emergency" conditions they were supposed to use a "special garbage bin" (Tabrizi 2004). As Nahid, a former inmate, described, "we took showers biweekly, and there were some

[5] A corridor that belonged to guards and the warden in Qasr prison.

showers in a dark, damp, and dirty room with slimy walls. The floor was always covered with dark and smelly water. Each block had just ten minutes to take a shower" (Tabrizi 2004, p. 122). Those prisoners who wrote a forgiveness request letter were considered as treasonous for being willing to cooperate with the regime; thereafter, they were isolated and excluded from all groups in the prison. As one prisoner in 1975 stated, "it seems there is one more cage around me. I wrote a forgiveness request letter to be released, and in turn I experienced prison inside the prison. Me and those prisoners who wrote forgiveness request letters were not allowed to express our ideas and suggestions in the *Komuns*. We were under the severe criticism of the *Komun*" (Tabrizi 2004, p. 163). Most celebrations, even traditional ones such as Nowruz, were banned by prisoners due to them being considered *shahane* ceremonies (kings' ceremonies) that should be avoided by communists (Tabrizi 2004, p. 207). All in all, women's political prisons in Mohammad Reza Shah's reign were like political schools. As Qezel Hesar's warden stated, "it was a school for training guerrillas and revolutionaries" (Tabrizi 2004, p. 209). The first time that incarcerated mothers were allowed to have in-person visits with their children was on March 21, 1976, in *Qasr* prison.

In 1975, the *Regulatory Code Governing Prisons and Affiliated Industrial and Agricultural Institutes* was published. It introduced six types of institutions for holding prisoners: detention centers, admission and diagnosis centers, closed prisons, semi-closed prisons, affiliated industrial and agricultural institutions, and juvenile correctional facilities. Although corporal punishment was not mentioned as a disciplinary measure in the 1975 regulatory code, excessive use of torture by the National Intelligence and Security Organization (SAVAK) was well documented during the reign of Mohammad Reza Shah. By the end of 1975, the regime had been criticized by international organizations due to the human rights abuses of SAVAK, and such incidents were detailed in a 1976 Amnesty International report. Thus, the regime banned torture and released the majority of political prisoners, with the number of political prisoners decreasing from 3000 in 1977 to 300 in 1979. For instance, out of 300 political prisoners in Qasr, 115 left (Tabrizi 2004). Also, the prison conditions improved dramatically; for instance, walls were painted, windows were changed, visiting hours were extended, the wire mesh was removed from visiting rooms, medical facilities were improved, and uncensored newspapers, books, TV, and radios were allowed (Abrahamian 1999). Women prisoners were even provided with two ping-pong tables in *Qasr* and allowed to prepare a wish list of books; however, guards and wardens gave a priority to religious books to intensify conflict and tensions between religious and non-religious prisoners (Tabrizi 2004). Evin had far more tolerable conditions than *Qasr* in terms of the structure, population, and social atmosphere. Women were kept in two large rooms with a door toward a green garden in contrast to the gray, small, dark, and overcrowded conditions of *Qasr*. Prisoners in Evin prison were more democratic. As one of the prisoners put it, "transferring from *Qasr* to Evin was like going on holiday" (Tabrizi 2004, p. 313). Nevertheless, Evin, like *Qasr*, changed its policies after a Red Cross site visit; prisoners were provided with audio players to listen to traditional music such as Shajarian and Lotfi and theater books such as "An Actor Prepares" by Konstantin Stanislavski to prepare prisoners for acting in a prison theater; all blocks' doors were kept open to let prisoners use the bathroom whenever they wanted, floors were carpeted, the use of cutlery not banned anymore, family visits were allowed two times a week, and family members were allowed to bring books and food for the prisoners (Tabrizi 2004).

The 1979 Revolution and Its Impact on Prison Conditions

In 1979, after 2500 years of monarchy, the last monarch of Iran, Mohammad Reza Pahlavi, was overthrown as a result of the Islamic Revolution and replaced by the Islamic Republic led by Ayatollah Ruhollah Khomeini with the slogan "neither the East nor the West, the Islamic government"; the regime considered itself as a representative of God on earth. While Reza Shah made an effort to restrict the role of clerics from the judiciary, the Islamic Republic Islamized the judiciary, conformed it to the sharia, and gave back the power to clerics and graduates of Islamic seminaries. In other words, one of the most important priorities of the new regime was to replace the previous penal code, which was based on the laws of western countries, with one based on sharia law.

Three bills regarding the Penal Code's amendment were passed by the Supreme Judicial Council and the Parliament in 1982: "the Law concerning *Hudud* and *Qisas*," "the Law concerning Islamic Punishments, General Provisions," and "the law concerning *Diyat*," which constituted the Islamic Penal Code, which contained four categories: *Hudud, qisas, Diyat*, and *Tazirat*. All *Hudud* (fixed penalties) criminals' acts (e.g. fornication, sodomy, lesbianism, pimping, drinking alcohol, robbery, terrorist acts, adultery) are subject to corporal punishment (e.g. flogging, cutting off limbs, execution, and stoning). Crimes such as intentional physical injuries and murder are subjected to retaliation or execution (*qisas*); however, unintentional physical injuries or even intentional physical injuries with forgiveness of the private plaintiff are subject to compensation or blood money (*Diyat*). *Tazirat* (discretionary punishment), including crimes against national security, insulting religious sanctions or state officials, personal insults, and offences against public morals, which are forbidden by *sharia* though the type and degree of punishment are not specified (i.e. there is no specific guideline, and it is in the hands of an Islamic judge and Islamic legislator), are subjected to discretionary punishments.

According to the 1979 prison regulations, prisons came under the control of the Ministry of Justice. In 1986, however, prisons and all their affiliated institutions were placed under the control of the Prisons Organization. Prisons before were governed and controlled by SAVAK, urban police, and the gendarmerie; however, in the Islamic Republic, prisons were centralized and governed by the council under the control of wardens, *Pasdars*, and clerical judges.

Following the Islamic Revolution, due to the *Dadgah-e Enqelab* (Revolutionary Tribunals) with the purpose of "cleansing society" of not only political activists but also non-political criminals (i.e. "this includes national security cases, such as those involving allegations of espionage, those involving political or civil activism, and drug-related offenses"), large number of victims were flogged, incarcerated, and executed (Amiry-Moghaddam 2018). About 260 non-political prisoners, including drug dealers, homosexuals, prostitutes, murderers, gamblers, and robbers, and

497 political prisoners were executed right after the revolution, and 7900 were executed from 1981 to 1985. Most of the drug dealers were hanged in public by Hojjat al-Islam Khalkhali, who was known as the "hanging judge" (Abrahamian 1999).

In the early period of the revolutionary transition, from 1979 to early 1981, when the Islamic Republic was settled, victims were not tortured. However, in 1981, when a political party (*Mujahidin*) attempted to overthrow the regime, torture became a common phenomenon in the prisons as a punishment, to get confessions, or to extract information regarding party leaders, safe houses, weapons, and so on. By 1983, major prisons were overcrowded by political and non-political prisoners. For instance, the capacity of *Komiteh* prison was 500, while there were 1500 inmates; the capacity of Evin was 1200, while there were 15,000 inmates; the capacity of *Qezel Hesar* was 10,000, while there were 15,000 inmates; the capacity of *Gohar Dasht* was 8000, while there were 16,000 inmates; and the capacity of *Qasr* was 1500, while there were 6000 inmates. To be more specific, by late 1981, Evin's cells were occupied by 75 prisoners instead of 15, *Qezel Hesar* by 48 instead of 18, and *Gohar Dasht* by 90 instead of 12 (Abrahamian 1999, pp. 125 & 169).

After the Islamic Revolution, Ayatollah Khomeini, "made it an absolute necessity to turn the prison into an educational institution, where Islam and the Revolution were dominant" (Carlsen 1982, pp. 147–148). In other words, all prisons became educational institutions, "rehabilitation centres," or "universities," where, according to Asad-o allah Lajevardi (Abrahamian 1999, p. 138), "deviants" were made into proper "human beings" or, as Rejali (1994, p. 118) put it, "where prisoners were taught the elements of good behaviours and the pains that are the rewards of evil conduct." This is still a prominent part of the Islamic regime, as prisoners are surrounded by excessive educational and training programs. Immediately after the revolution, prisoners constantly received religious training from prison ideological sessions, loudspeakers in cells and yards, compulsory congregational prayers, radio, TV, and newspapers to persuade them to change or repent. Watching religious programs on television was compulsory, especially once *tawabs* were around (Parvaresh 2007). However, educational training was not limited to those programs, as keeping *tawabin* in prison while they repented was another tool used to educate prisoners. Prisoners were supposed to fast during *Ramadan* and pray, except for non-Muslims and women who were menstruating; otherwise, they were flogged. Additionally, under the Lajevardi[6] control over Evin prison, even celebrating *Nowruz* was forbidden. Prisoners were supposed to be cautious about the *najis* rules, which forbid Muslims from coming into physical contact with those who were ritually impure (e.g. Christians, Jews, leftists, and Bahais). Conditions for women in prisons were even worse due to the new compulsory black *chador* rule and a high sensitivity toward women's sexuality, which resulted in women coming under the microscope.

For all *jadidi* (newcomers) in Evin, if they were lucky, one or two weeks after their arrival, they were provided with two military blankets—one to be used as a mattress and the other as a cover. Meanwhile, prisoners had to share what was available in their cells. One of the former prisoners stated that they suffered from a lack of basic toiletries such as toothbrushes, toothpaste, shampoo, and hairbrushes, which forced them to use the leftovers of former prisoners. In a best-case scenario, they were provided with one bar of soap and a box of sanitary pads monthly. Also, in Evin prison, there were only six toilets for 300 prisoners (Agah et al. 2007). The prisoners had a daily routine. They woke up at 6:30 am and collected all the blankets and folded them in the corner to be used as a sofa during the day. They had breakfast at 7:30 am, which was usually three sugar cubes, tea, a tiny piece of feta cheese, and a package of flat bread that was meant to be split among the cell occupants. After breakfast, some inmates exercised by walking forward and backward, jumping up and down, and stretching, while others participated in language classes, chatted with friends, watched television, washed clothes, did crossword puzzle, or clipped their nails. They also participated in an "educational program" after breakfast, which included Islamic training and a so-called self-defamation ritual. Lunch and dinner were almost the same; however, dinner was lighter such as bread with jam or butter or a potato or hard-boiled egg, which was occasionally replaced by a "weekly

[6] Sayyid Assadollah Ladjevardi was a political prisoner before the Islamic Revolution. In 1979, he was given a post as the chief prosecutor of Tehran. In 1981, he was appointed as the warden of Evin. According to Abrahamian (1999, p. 136), he "liked to be addressed as Hajj Aqa, and boasted he was so proud of Evin that he had brought his family to live there."

report" soup that contained all the foods left over from the week. After dinner, the prisoners were involved in different activities such as watching TV, socializing, mending clothes, and preparing the "beds." Those inmates who had been brutally tortured, were giving birth to a child, or were in danger of committing suicide were put on the priority list for seeing a doctor; otherwise, the waiting time was several months (Agah et al. 2007).

Prisoners were under constant surveillance of neither guards nor the warden, but rather *tawabin* (repentants) who were intended to disclose any secret information about their cellmates or even friends in return for incentives (e.g. early release or working in the workshops to earn money). Most *Tawabin*, as Agah et al. (2007) states, were informants or collaborators of wardens and guards; as informants in prison, they were assigned to spy on those who disobeyed the religious authorities; in other words, they were figures in the hands of the state to enforce religious beliefs among unbelievers to turn prisons into Muslim universities. As Agah et al. (2007, p. 50) stated, "I hate *tawabs*; whatever we do and say is reported to the office by them. You have to be careful with your relationships. You show your beliefs by choosing who you spend your time with or talk to." Despite the efforts of guards and wardens to break solidarity, especially among political prisoners through assigning *tawabs* among prisoners, almost all former prisoners who were incarcerated after the revolution described a spirit of sympathy and support among prisoners, as demonstrated by sharing budgets, sleeping spaces, clothes, basic toiletries, and food as well as taking care of children, especially for those who were transferred into other wards, pregnant women, sick prisoners, and mothers with children.

> *Political prisoners support each other so much so that they were a model for criminals. Even the criminals who scared everyone in the ward respected them and came to them for advice.* (Female participant, two years of incarceration)

Prisoners had restricted access to the outside world. They were only provided with government newspapers, the content of which were monitored. As Agah et al. (2007) described, even those newspapers were not distributed on a large scale, and one inmate usually read it aloud to everyone. Those prisoners who were allowed to have family visits were supposed to speak Farsi[7]and the visits were limited to ten minutes only.

> *I told the guards that I cannot speak Farsi with my sister. I spoke with them in our own language as far as I remember. But, they did not care. They wanted to listen to our chats to control everything.* (Female participant, two years of incarceration)

Additionally, prisoners suffered from shortages of food and medicine from 1980 to 1988 during the Iran-Iraq War. For instance, in Marand prison, which was located beneath a building, there was no yard for walking or kitchen for preparing food. Instead, prisoners received 20 Toman daily, while one dish of food was 30 Toman (Abdi 2011).

The wardens and guards used *tawab* recruited from the ranks of prisoners to not only disrupt the solidarity but also create a hierarchy, which resulted in tensions and conflict. In these circumstances, many of those who could not tolerate the intense pressure committed suicide. Nevertheless, prisoners attempted to entertain themselves through different activities, from walking in the yards, chatting with friends, reading books and newspapers, watching TV, listening to the radio, and learning English, Arabic, Kurdish, and French. Prisoners from the same political party tried to live together in the same cells to not only share thoughts, but also food, cigarettes, money, and assistance. The administrators of prisons were in charge of the direct control and surveillance of the wards, and the leaders of each cell were selected by them to distribute food, manage the finances, manage shower times, assign workers each day to clean cells and wash dishes,[8] allocate sleeping spaces, and transfer all messages from the wards to the prisoners and vice versa.

In 1984, the widespread use of torture in Iranian prisons caused severe criticism of the Islamic Republic of Iran from the part of human rights organizations. As a result, prison conditions were improved by released

[7] Ethnic groups in Iran are mostly recognized by their language and religion. Although more than 50% of the population in Iran are Persian speakers and 99% of the population in Iran are Muslim, there are 27 ethnic groups in Iran who speak a different language and have a different religion (e.g. Kurds, Arabs, Baluches) (Amanolahi 2005).

[8] Every day, one inmate was responsible for cleaning up the cell.

repenters who wrote "letters of regret,"[9] helping prisoners receive better quality food and warm clothes, providing educational facilities for those who were interested in continuing their education, allowing inmates to have group recreation activities such as volleyball and soccer, increasing family visit times, and lifting restrictions on reading some non-religious books such as Molavi (a poet) and "War and Peace" by Leo Tolstoy. Despite these improvements, each cell in Evin prison was still only equipped with four washrooms and three bathrooms for 50 prisoners, and the prisoners were only allowed to use them three times daily and 15 minutes each time. In 1982, there was just one washroom for 100 inmates in each cell. Furthermore, in 1982, the occupants of each cell were divided into two groups to manage their sleeping time: one group slept from 11:00 pm to 7:00 am, and the other group slept from the morning to the afternoon. Since the prison cells expanded in 1984, all the inmates could sleep at the same time—albeit there was no room left for turning aside. Overcrowding, inadequate access to washrooms and bathrooms, unhygienic conditions, and poor food and health quality are well described as occurring in prisons in Iran.

In 1993, *Adelabad* prison, a major prison in Shiraz that kept serious criminals, gave "the drug addicts a particularly hard time… [T]hey were not prescribed any drugs or given any medical treatment, so they would sometimes shake uncontrollably and scream in agony as they suffered the effects of withdrawal. We could help them as best we could, but they needed proper medical attention, and we could only offer them friendship" (Roohizadegan 1993). In 1999, the quarantine ward in Evin prison housed 1000 prisoners with two washrooms, and most of the prisoners slept in corridors, hallways, and cell floors (Sehati 2009).

Prison regulations were updated in 2005[10] and extended to 247 articles. The amended regulations divided prisons into two categories: closed prisons (i.e. institutions protected by walls, guard towers, and with internal and external protection) and vocational training and occupational camps (i.e. institutions where prisoners work during the day and

[9] Inmates who repented their "sins" or "crimes," especially political prisoners.

[10] It was another short period of reforming prison, which was followed by an international conference on Reducing the Use of Incarceration in June 2007 (Tehran, Iran).

return to their sleeping quarters at night). According to the 2005 prison regulations, as the previous regulatory code, prisoners should be provided with a breakfast, lunch, and dinner that contains bread, cheese, and tea for breakfast and vegetables, rice, potatoes, onions, legumes, dairy products, eggs, and fruit for lunch and dinner. The prisons should be equipped with a sufficient number of showers so that prisoners can take a shower at least once a week. The prisons should provide prisoners with the opportunity to continue their education, and literacy classes should be made available to illiterate inmates under the age of 60. According to the International Center for Prison Studies, there were 217,851 prisoners in temporary detention areas and prisons, 163,000 of whom were incarcerated in prisons and considered as having the potential to be enrolled in employment and educational or vocational training. While, according to Iran's cooperation foundation, approximately 58,788 prisoners were involved in those training programs in 2012 (Iran Human Rights, 2015).

However, in 2011, *Andarzgah* ward in *Qezel Hesar* was equipped with four or five showers for 200 prisoners, and, as a result of overcrowding, prisoners could take a shower only once a week. Also, the prison was overrun with lice and had no heating or air conditioning equipment (Kantoori 2011). Also, the quarantine ward in *Vakilabad* prison in Mashhad, which had a capacity of 25 prisoners, was occupied with almost 80 inmates, and those prisoners who worked in the prison factories were paid 5000 toumans[11] monthly, while workers outside of the prison received 8000 toumans hourly for the same job (Ghaderi 2013b). In 2012, 13-meter cells in Isfahan central prison with 10 three-store beds held 55 to 77 prisoners; only 30 of them could sleep on the beds, and the rest slept on the floor. The situation was even worse for addict criminals since 40 of them had to squeeze into the small quarantine areas for a couple of days before being transferred to the prison. Most of the facilities (e.g. fridges and television) in the cells were provided by wealthy prisoners. The same was true for sleeping facilities such as blankets; otherwise, military blankets were the only options they could have. There

[11] US$0.33.

were eight bathrooms for 300 prisoners in the *band-e-nesvan* (women's section) of Isfahan central prison.

According to Abdi (2011), every two minutes, one person was incarcerated during the period between 1980 and 1986, and in less than six years, the prison population increased by 91%. The prison population in Iran increased sharply from 14,019[12] in 1980 to 296,565 in 1986. Although 47% of the population in prisons were drug-related criminals, this number increased to 63% in 1986; in other words, the number of drug-related criminals increased by 134% from 1982 to 1988. The prison population increased by 97%, from 118 prisoners for every 100,000 people in 1988 to 232 prisoners for every 100,000 people in 2010 (Table 2.1).

The growing number of people incarcerated in Iran is due to considering incarceration as an alternative to other forms of punishment (e.g. flogging), changing and intensifying laws regarding some crimes (e.g. drug-related crimes), and the increasing number of political prisoners. Although prisons' conditions were improved, the growing number of prisoners and overcrowding after the Islamic Revolution turned the so-called university, which had the goal of making "human beings," into a "recidivism workshop."

Table 2.1 Prison population trend up to 2018, published in *World Prison Brief*, Institute for Crime & Justice Policy Research

Year	Prison population total	Prison population rate (per 100,000 of national population)
1980	10,000	26
1993	101,801	172
2001	158,000	237
2003	157,267	229
2005	134,384	192
2007	148,843	207
2009	168,514	229
2011	250,000	331
2013	226,000	294
2018	240,000	294

[12] Although some of the numbers about prison population in Iran published in a book titled "Prison's Impact on Prisoners" written by Abbas Abdi (2011) is different from the ones in the World Prison Brief, the author preferred to keep both to demonstrate the differences.

References

Abbasi, Z. (2012). God's Law V. Corporations: A Critique of Islamic Law Matters Thesis.

Abdi, A. (2011). *Tasir-E Zendan Bar Zendani, Entesharati Nour*, Tehran.

Abrahamian, E. (1982). *Iran between two revolutions*. Princeton University Press.

Abrahamian, E. (1999). *Tortured confessions: Prisons and public recantations in modern Iran*. Univ of California Press.

Adamiyat, F., & Nāteq, H. (1977). *Afkar-I Ijtimai Va Siyasi Va Iqtisadi: Dar Asar-I Muntashir-Nashudah-'I Duran-I Qajar*. Agah.

Agah, A., Mehr, S., & Parsi, S. (2007). *We Lived to Tell: Political Prison Memoirs of Iranian Women*. McGilligan Books Inc.

Amanat, A. (2009). *Apocalyptic Islam And Iranian Shi'ism*. IB Tauris; New York: Distributed in the US By Palgrave Macmillan.

Amanolahi, S. (2005). A Note on Ethnicity and Ethnic Groups in Iran. *Iran & The Caucasus*, 37–41.

Amiry-Moghaddam, M. (2018). The Globe Post. Retrieved from https://Theglobepost.Com/2018/02/22/Iran-Revolutionary-Courts/.

Amoui, M. (1993). *Dard-E Zendan: Khaterat-E Mohammad Ali Amoui*. Tehran.

Ansari, S. (1996). *Az Zendegiy-E Man*. Los Angeles.

Avanessian, A. (1979). *Yadashthay-e Zendan Salhay-e* 1928–1942.

Bakhash, S. (1978). Iran: Monarchy, Bureaucracy & Reform Under The Qajars, 1858–1896 (Vol. 8). Middle East Centre, St. Antony's College.

Baqeyi, G. (1994). *Khaterat Az Doran-E Faaliyat-E Hezbe Tudeh*. Tehran.

Carlsen, R. W. (1982). *The Imam and His Islamic Revolution: A Journey into Heaven and Hell.* Snow Man Press.

Curzon, G. N. (1966). *Persia and the Persian Question* (2 Vols., Repr.). London: Frank Cass & Co.

Daneshvar, P. (2016). *Revolution in Iran*. Springer.

Eftekhari, Y. (1991). *Khaterat-e Dowran-e Separishud-e*. (Memories Of A Begone Era).

Enayat, H. (2005). *Modern Islamic Political Thought*. IB Tauris.

Enayat, H. (2013). The New Legal Institutions in Practice, 1906–1941. In *Law, State, and Society in Modern Iran* (pp. 145–173). New York: Palgrave Macmillan.

Entessar, N. (1988). *Criminal Law and the Legal System in Revolutionary Iran*. BC Third World.

Etemadzade, M. (1991). *Mehman-e Baradaran*. Tehran.

Ghaderi, S. (2013b). *Witness Statement of Siamak Ghaderi*. Iran Human Rights Documentation Center (IHRDC).
Haghi, B. (1993). *Lahazati Az Zendegiy-E Safar Ghahramaniyan. Nashr-E Azarbayehjan*.
Hamidian, N. (2010). *Safar Ba Balhaye Arezo.*. Stockholm.
Hosseini, M. (1991). *Zendan Va Zendani Dar Iran*. Ganjineh.
Iran Human Rights. (2015). Rights Disregarded: Prisons in the Islamic Republic of Iran.
Kantoori, A. (2011). *Witness Statement of Ali Kantoori*. Iran Human Rights Documentation Center (IHRDC).
Kasravi, A. (1942). *Parcham* Newspaper, Number 159.
Kasravi, A. (2004). *Tarikh-E Mashrot-E Iran*. Tehran: Amir Kabir.
Keshavarz, K. (1984). *Chahardah Mah Dark Khark: Yaddashthaye Rozane-Ye Zendani*. Tehran: Payam Publisher.
Khameyi, A. (1993). *Forsat-E Bozorg-E Az Dast Raft-E*. Tehran: Hafte Publisher.
Lotfi, Y. (2013). *Falak-O Alaflak: Zendan-E Sard-E Pahlavi. Mozeh Ebrat-E*. Iran.
Madani, Said. (2006, November 7). The Evolution of Prisoners' Rights from the Constitutional Revolution to the Present Day. *Etemad-E Melli*.
Majdoleslam Kermani, A. (1971). *Tarikhe-Enghelabe-Mashrotiyat-E Iran*. Isfahan: Isfahan University.
Maleki, Kh. (1956). *Zendan-E Falak Al-Falak*. *Ferdosi* Journal. Tehran.
Mazaheri, A. (2005). *Shekofehay-E Derakht-E Anar:* 4791 Days in *Shahanshahi* Prison.
Mokhtari, P. (1950). Tarikh-e Haftad sal-e Plic-e Iran. Artesh publisher.
Motadel, D. (2011). Qajar Shahs in Imperial Germany. *Past & Present, 213*(1), 191–235.
Ovanessian, A. (1944). *Yaddasht-ha-ye Zendan*. Tehran.
Parvaresh, N. (2007). *Nabardi Nabarabar:* Report of Seven Years in Prison. *Andish-e And Peykar*.
Pishevari, J. (1944). *Yaddasht-haye Zendan.*, Tehran
Raffat, D. (1985). *The Prison Papers of Bozorg Alavi: A Literary Odyssey*. Syracuse University Press.
Rahami, M. (2005). Development of criminal punishment in the Iranian post revolutionary penal code. *European Journal of Crime, Criminal Law and Criminal Justice, 13*(4), 585–602.
Rahnama, M. (2013). *Yazdah Mah Dar Khark. Soreh Mehr Entesharat*.
Rejali, D. M. (1994). *Torture and modernity: Self, society, and state in modern Iran*. Westview.

Roohizadegan, O. (1993). *Olya's Story: A Survivor's Dramatic Account of the Persecution of Bahá'ís in Revolutionary Iran*. One World Publications Limited.
Sayah Mahalati, M. (1988). *Khaterat-E Haj Sayah Ya Dorey-E Khof Va Vahshat. Ebn-E Sina*, Tehran.
Sehati, K. (2009). *Witness Statement: Kourosh Sehati*. Iran Human Rights Documentation Center (IHRDC).
Shaghaghi, M. (1974). *Khaterat-E Momtahen-O Aldol-E*. Tehran: Amirkabir.
Shirali, M. (2017). *The Mystery of Contemporary Iran*. Routledge.
Tabrizi, V. (2004). *Dad-E Bidad*. First Women Political Prisoners, Forough Book.
Tajolsaltane. (1982). *Khaterat-E Taj-O Alsaltane. Nashr-E Tarikh-E Iran*, Tehran.
Tavana, M. H. (2014). Three Decades of Islamic Criminal Law Legislation in Iran: A Legislative History Analysis with Emphasis on the Amendments of the 2013 Islamic Penal Code. *Electronic Journal of Islamic and Middle Eastern Law (EJIMEL), 2*(9), 24–38.
Werner, C. (2000). *An Iranian Town in Transition: A Social and Economic History of the Elites of Tabriz, 1747–1848* (Vol. 1). Otto Harrassowitz Verlag.

3

Prison Subculture

A prison is a self-contained world (Clemmer 1940), or as Oleinik (2003) states, it is a "small society" that has its own structural criteria that are vastly different from the rest of society. According to Clemmer (1958, p. 299), every offender who enters a prison is affected by prisonization to some extent. New entrants have to be ready to accept a subordinate role, develop new habits of eating, dressing, working, and sleeping, and adapt to the new patterns of language.

Prison community provides an opportunity for prisoners to constitute a social system and expand the informal social order, which differs from the social order commanded by the officers. Prisoners are a mass of isolated individuals that are aggregated instead of being a social group or a society. Prison is shaped by its surrounding social environment and reflects the state's dominant ideology. For Foucault (1979), prison is not an isolated building in the city; rather, it is integrated into the city. It does not exist in isolation, and its institution and setting are mixed with that of its surrounding society despite the definite boundary of the prison's walls: "It appears that total institutions do not substitute their own unique culture for something already formed: we deal with something more restricted than acculturation or assimilation" (Goffman 1961, p. 13).

N. R. Anaraki, *Prison in Iran*, Palgrave Studies in Prisons and Penology,
https://doi.org/10.1007/978-3-030-57169-6_3

In fact, "disculturation" happens in prison, which involves "untraining which renders him temporarily incapable of managing certain features of daily life on the outside, if and when he gets back to it" (Goffman 1961, p. 13). Additionally, the degradation ceremony on the first day of entering the total institution strips away the inmates' name, usual appearance, and identity, a process that Goffman refers to as the "mortification of self." It is important to consider that prisonization is the intermittent social process in prison. That is, during the process of the mortification of self and disculturation, some parts of an inmate's identity remain intact. According to Goffman (1961, p. 12), prisoners come to prison with a "presenting culture" that has emerged from their "home world."

Prisonization provides opportunities for offenders to become aware of the values and norms of criminals. As Oleinik (2013) states, for offenders who are convicted of drug-related crimes, prison plays a principal role in resocialization. This situation can be made worse by group imprisonment. The Islamic Republic of Iran keeps most of its convicts in groups. The incarceration of drug-related offenders affects their lives after prison not only because of becoming familiarized with the prison subculture, but also because it makes the desistance process more complicated. Seven categories were extracted from the data to explain the subculture of prisons in Iran: (1) unstable pyramid, (2) captive as a society, (3) battle zone, (4) hegemony of drug-related networks, (5) multiple identities, (6) instrumental relationships, and (7) two sides of the same coin.

Unstable Pyramid

According to Sykes (1958), the main goal of a prison code is maintaining prison solidarity and cohesion. Thus, the more the inmates adopt the prison code, the more the stability and solidarity between prisoners is guaranteed; otherwise, a "war of all against all" will be inevitable. However, in Iranian prisons, adopting informal rules causes solidarity and instability simultaneously. Prison stability is manipulated through three different routes: (1) Informal prison rules are disobeyed by inmates on different occasions; for instance, members of gangs do not always support other members in committing violent acts and try not to put their safety in jeopardy, which undermines the cohesion of the gang. In other cases, inmates do not always respect the king of the prison (*Vakil Band*), and some prisoners use physical violence, even against those with dominant status, and defeat him/her, which results in changing the dominant groups, changing social orders, and subsequently shaking the solidarity skeleton. Most often, this challenges the general roles of prison; (2) Gangs are the second route for challenging solidarity, as power struggles pit gangs against one another to take authority in the prison. Prisoners do not always show respect for the rules and norms established by the dominant gangs; (3) One of the most important reasons for instability in the pyramid in prison is the recruiting of informants by prison administration. Informants transfer security-related information, which results in decreasing loyalty and trust among prisoners. An overwhelming lack of solidarity and the social dynamics of the prison atmosphere put prisoners in an emergency zone in which social orders are produced and reproduced constantly.

Thus, dominant status is not static or fixed in prison and hierarchy criteria seem to change over time, since social orders follow the negotiations of social construction and social orders and norms are transformed by changing those who control resources and make decisions in the prison. Living in an unstable/shifting zone in which nobody can be a king forever pushes prisoners to have to face the constant challenge of adapting to new orders and norms once the dominant group is changed.

> *We have to admit that the dominant group in the prison was not stable. Likewise, in society, everything is updated every day. The criminal skills and drugs are being changed over time. When I was incarcerated, we did not know about methamphetamine, but during recent years, young people from the wealthy regions of the city who are familiar with new drugs and new forms of crimes are the dominant group in the prison. Forms of managing the prison, even fighting, languages, everything, are being changed gradually. Sometimes, a group of prisoners will set up a fight with the dominant group in the prison, and if they win, they take their position, then all the prisoners will be under their wing. What I mean is that managing is not in the hands of one group always; it has been changing as time passes.* (Male participant, nine years of incarceration)

The clash between conflicting identities in a total institution is not just a struggle between the previous identity and the institutional identity, but also the "yesterday" identity and the "tomorrow" one. This means that prisoners feel like they are living in quicksand, requiring constant adjustments to new orders; this is true even for long-termers. Or as Liebling (2013, p. 23) states, "prisoners described a crisis of identity and a crisis of recognition." For dominant groups to fulfill their aims and govern inmates in a full manner, cooperation must be obtained from prisoners through highlighting the new informal code of conduct. The challenge of adapting to the new sets of rules pushes them toward a multiple identity. Although criminologists believe that the former identity of inmates gradually deteriorates during incarceration periods, the results of my study reveal that incarcerated addicts have constant struggles due to changing identities. The former and previous identities neither deteriorate nor are stripped; rather, they fade, but they remain alive.

Inmates are exposed to unstable or even contradictory circumstances. Once they are incarcerated, they must manage the inner conflict between the orders of the outside and inside worlds, even if they were used to a criminal lifestyle before incarceration. The circumstances can be more challenging for drug users who are not familiar with the criminal subculture, as they have not necessarily been in contact with criminals. Once they are incarcerated because of possessing 30 grams of heroin, they will be sentenced to death, requiring them to live in prison as their second and last home and adopt an institutional identity.

If you are just a drug abuser, you are nothing in the prison. You must be a criminal and drug dealer to change others' minds toward you. Once I was imprisoned, I was like trash; nobody communicated with me. I did not even know how to talk and with whom to talk. I did not know how to manage my life among those criminals. I was scared. I did not belong to this place. I was just a drug user who carried 30 grams of heroin for my own usage. I was shocked once I heard about the sexual relationships between women in the prison. I just could not believe how it might be possible. I heard about the drug trafficking in the prison, but I did not see it. I slept in the corridors. I did not see anything. I was not allowed to see anything. They assaulted each other constantly. The words were so strange to me. It took months and months for me to get used to this situation. I tried to put aside everything that I knew and started from scratch. (Female participant, two years of incarceration)

Some of the prisoners, especially incarcerated women, are incarcerated and sentenced to the death penalty just because of trafficking drugs in order to provide for their children. Most of them are the principal breadwinners of the family who were abandoned by drug addict husbands. The only dreams they had were to raise and feed their children and save them from misery.

I was arrested for delivering one kilogram of heroin from Bandar Abbas to Isfahan to afford to live. I have seven children whose lives are in my hands. I was the breadwinner of my home, as my husband was an addict, and he abandoned us three years ago. I was addicted to opium myself, but it was pervasive and usual in our tribe that people use opium. I did not know anything about crimes and criminals. One day I decided to do something for my children to make them happy, because I could not afford even their food. My sister had five children and her husband was also addicted. She and I decided to transfer drugs to another city, and in return, we were promised that we would earn 500,000 toman.[1] *That was so much money for us. We did it, but we got arrested in Isfahan. I cannot forget the day my sister and I got imprisoned in the central prison of Isfahan. We did not know anything; I mean, anything about the life in the prison. We were scared to the extent that when we entered the prison, we did not even go to the yard for one month. My sister, she's older than me, she told the guards that we didn't know how to survive in this place and asked them to help us. As time passed, every day we changed. We each became another person. We still have difficulties getting used to the prison life because it is completely new in our lives. I did not know how to find drugs in the prison, I did not even know that you could find it in the prison easier than outside. I was a mother, and I had seven children. How could I deal with criminals every second? Those challenges made me crazy. The day the judge told us you are sentenced to the death penalty, we fell on the floor. We are on death row now after five years of living in prison and I barely see my children. I have to say that it is not our place; it is not.* (Female participant, nine years of incarceration)

[1] US$33.

Even murderers declared that they did not have regular contact with the criminal culture before being incarcerated. Most of the incarcerated drug addicts were involved in violent acts while they were high on drugs, not because they had a predefined plan to murder someone. Thus, this indicates that almost all of them were not familiar with the criminal code of behavior before being imprisoned.

> *It is true that I am a murderer, but I did not have constant communication with criminals. I was addicted to heroin and when I was high, I killed my friend in a fight. I entered the prison and did not know what to do. I was a murderer and all the prisoners expected me to act as a murderer, but I did not. I was not a murderer. I did not know how murderers act or behave. My personality was torn apart. I lost myself. Every second in the prison I reminded myself that you are in the prison and must act as a murderer. You are not outside. These struggles still follow me, even now after 9 years.* (Male participant, nine years of incarceration)

Prisoners are dealing with unstable and contradictory circumstances simultaneously; the contradiction is not limited only to the inner contradiction between the previous identity and the continuous new ones. However, the contradictory criteria of hierarchy push prisoners to show respect toward the conflicting identities in the prison. Violent criminals who are brutal, financially independent, managers of the cells, and powerful enough to control drug networks must be respected. Also, prisoners who are innocent, sources of calmness, seniors, *loti* (being honorable and high-minded), and mediators *(rish sefid)* should be respected as well. Thus, the accumulation of contradictions leads prisoners to live in a "limbo" and always be ready to act contradictorily.

Different studies have been conducted regarding the inevitability of informal hierarchical organizations emerging within total institutions (e.g. Crewe 2005; Trammell 2012; Garabedian 1963). The status of prisoners is determined based on seven factors: (1) criminal history, (2) controlling drug networks, (3) wealth, (4) spiritual identity, (5) social capital, (6) sexuality, and (7) loyalty.

Criminal History

It is well documented that criminal history is a principal factor through which the status of inmates is determined (Vaughn and Sapp 1989; West 1983). Violent criminals (e.g. murderers and drug traffickers) have higher status, authority, and control, which differentiate them from others.

> *Someone who got imprisoned because of trafficking a considerable amount of drugs received respect.* (Male participant, four years of incarceration)

Although newcomers in the prison were not even seen as human beings, those who were incarcerated because of murder or drug trafficking were respected once they entered the prison.

> *My cellmate was incarcerated for trafficking one tonne of illegal drugs. She was a king in the prison. Nobody dared treat her with anything other than respect. That was enough for her to become a new boss in the prison. She entered the prison one day and became our boss the next day.* (Female participant, four years of incarceration)

> *Like all organizations in society, the prison has a hierarchy. The most violent criminals with long-term incarceration will be a manager and boss of 400 prisoners in one section of the prison. So, all prisoners are under his command. Like ordinary life outside the prison that requires emotion, money, and affection, the boss of the section demands all of these from the prisoners. Prisoners who are under his control must provide all those to them. You have to be a victim in the prison or try hard to gain power to be a boss.* (Male participant, nine years of incarceration)

Particular types of offences such as *dale dozdi* (petty robbery), and *khorde forosh* (small-scale drug dealing) degrade the inmates' status in the eyes of other inmates. In general, non-violent criminals have low status, especially if they do not have any personal possessions (e.g. money, drugs for personal use, or cigarettes). Also, street drug addicts who were incarcerated due to petty offences (i.e. consuming drugs or possessing drugs) were afforded the least exclusive lifestyle.

> *Those who were incarcerated because of minor drug offences had no respect. Someone who did a petty crime was treated as a piece of shit. They even do not have a bed for sleeping, so they must sleep in the washrooms. Washrooms for petty crimes.* (Male participant, six years of incarceration)

> *I was just a drug user. I was weak, and I was not even able to talk. Attention and ideas toward drug users who were criminals as well were completely different. If I had entered the prison as a criminal who was addicted as well, everything would have been different. I was in a bad physical situation. I had a lot of pain, and, I was emotionally weak and vulnerable. Most prisoners were criminals. They were not the same as me at all. I wished I was a criminal or drug trafficker, so I could have a better life in the prison. I had nothing, just pain in the prison.* (Female participant, one year of incarceration)

Most drug users who got incarcerated because of abusing drugs or possessing drugs were "silent" victims in prison. They were tortured not only by society but also by prisoners in the smaller society; in their own words, "*they did not belong to prison.*" Most of them had constant contact with their providers or with other people who use drugs on the street; they were not directly involved in any criminal activities.

> *I used drugs in our neighborhoods with my friends. We slept in the street, but in a specific part of the town with specific rules. I remember the day I wanted to change my street and go somewhere else to sleep. My friends in the street told me that you must stay here because in this place, we know you and your father. If you know the person's background, you can communicate with them. It is not the same in other streets. You cannot know about their criminal histories. You should not communicate with them. Whatever we do in the street, at least we are not criminals. We just use drugs and sell drugs. Once I was incarcerated, I told myself that the street was safer than the prison. I did not expect this many murderers or drug traffickers in one place. I was addicted to methamphetamine, and despite all the connections I had in the street with people who use drugs, I could not find drugs in the prison because I did not know anything about the prison and their connections. If you do not know anything or anybody in the prison, nobody cares about you. They just live their own life. They simply ignore you. I did not even have a place to sleep. In the drug units, prisoners do not have enough beds, clothes, and food. The only thing you can find in large quantities was drugs. Thus, if you are a poor drug abuser with no criminal skills and no*

connections, you must sleep in washrooms and corridors. There is not enough food, so mostly you will be hungry. You will not even have any spare clothes. This is the situation of people who use drugs in the prison. (Female participant, two years of incarceration)

Most addicted women claimed that they created a small prison for themselves by not seeing close family members and people in society during the time they were addicted. Most of them do not have any contact with criminals and offenders even to buy drugs. In fact, their close family members or boyfriends provide them with drugs to keep them hidden at home to protect their "honor." As a result, they were not familiar with the criminal culture before being incarcerated, as they were incarcerated at their own home beforehand.

My husband told me repeatedly to just stay at home and let me know if you need drugs. I was threatened several times, as he said that if I leave the house, he will kill me. He told me that I embarrassed him. He provided me with drugs for more than 10 years. I did not even see my provider myself. But nobody cared about me in the prison. They did not consider me a human being. I was like trash or garbage to them. I begged them to give me drugs or food, but none of them would look at me. (Female participant, one year of incarceration)

Inmates sentenced to death or life imprisonment were called *saheb-khane* (landlord). The status of an inmate who has been in prison for 3 years is higher than an inmate who has been there for 12 months. Inmates with less than 6-month sentences are not just incarcerated and isolated from the outside community but also from the inner prison world. Thus, they become double outcasts and the waste of the wasted. Most drug traffickers and murderers who were long-termers are knowledgeable enough regarding the social actions in the prison structure, and their knowledge gives them power to oppress others. The prison social structure invests in violent criminals who are permanent residents of the prison. Short-termers, especially poor and addicted ones, are not worth investing in; they are considered strangers who will leave this home before getting anything from the prison culture but degradation, fear, dehumanization, and being addicted to methadone.

> *There was a prisoner who was incarcerated for 20 years; he had dignity and respect. I was not scared of him; actually, I respected him because he was forced to live in the most difficult situation in the prison for 20 years. In fact, we respected his incarceration length and his broad knowledge about prison life. There was a difference between someone who was incarcerated for 6 months and someone with 20 years' incarceration. Prison has a tough atmosphere. They deserve respect. For example, you have to respect the older ones who have been incarcerated for a long time in the bathroom and washroom line. That did not mean that we were scared; we just respected their age, experiences, knowledge, and length of incarceration.* (Male participant, nine years of incarceration)

Inmates with longer sentences play a key role for inmates and correctional officers simultaneously (this will be explained in detail in a section entitled "Two Sides of the Same Coin"). They exercise informal power in managing and controlling the prison and are usually recruited by high-status prisoners and correctional officers to act as a *nemayande* (representative or leader) of units.

> *Prisoners who had committed the most violent crimes will be sentenced to life imprisonment or the death penalty, so they act as a boss in the units (nemayande).* (Male participant, four years of incarceration)

> *Even managing the prison depends on the criminal history of prisoners. Sometimes we witnessed that 50 prisoners who are gang members managed 10,000 prisoners, just because two or three of them have been the most violent criminals in the prison, so they were selected through leaders or officers to act as a manager.* (Male participant, nine years of incarceration)

One of the requirements for being considered a powerful and high-status inmate is having adequate knowledge about prison relations, values, norms, rules, codes, orders, and obligations. Possessing information brings safety, drugs, and status; for instance, being knowledgeable about drug networks in the prison provides opportunities for prisoners to access drugs safely and securely. To be aware of different aspects of the prison's structure requires a long-term incarceration experience, which creates social capital in the prison. Being in prison for several years assists prisoners in getting to know the social structure of prison and building social ties with prisoners, which leads to obtaining knowledge. Since inmates with longer sentences are considered "invisible managers" of the prison, all drug importing is done under their constant surveillance. Prisoners are not allowed simply to transfer drugs to the prison without getting permission; prisoners who do not have high status in the prison have to get permission and then share drugs with the invisible managers as a token of obedience. Newcomers in the prison, especially drug users with no criminal history, have a lack of knowledge about the organization, which increases their vulnerability.

> *I was just a drug user when I was incarcerated, and I did not engage in any criminal activity. Once I got imprisoned, I did not even know how to get drugs for my own use in the prison. I did not know anyone or anywhere in the prison. I was there for 45 days, and I was so weak. Sometimes one woman in the next cell talked to me and gave me food; otherwise, nobody gave me even one gram of any kind of drug.* (Female participant, one year of incarceration)

> *They know everything about the prison; you just have to ask them. You become a master just by spending some months in the prison. You cannot imagine what has happened to someone who has spent 9 years in prison. They are the landlord. They are the president. They are the bosses.* (Male participant, nine years of incarceration)

The most sensitive and high-security positions in prison are assigned to high-status inmates. In fact, they have already carried the title of violent criminals, and they have been equipped with another title (high-status job position), which subsequently doubles their respect and criminal activities in the prison.

> *I got the best job in the prison since the duration of my incarceration was long. For example, we were mediators between the outside and inside of the prison. There was a possibility that prisoners who were not violent criminals and were not sentenced to long incarcerations were offered this type of position, but it completely depended on their criminal record and their behaviours in the prison; there was a metaphor in the prison that 'nobody should feel the smell of your mouth' (do not say any inappropriate, unnecessary, or impolite words). We were addicted to heroin in the prison, but we did not engage in any violent*

behaviour or bullying in the prison. We minded our own business. As a result, we were mediators in the health section in the prison. Our duties were filling out the basic health information forms for new prisoners and taking appointments with physicians for them in the prison. All the responsibilities of taking care of medicine and pills were on us. We always misused our opportunities and our position. We were also responsible for giving loratin to heavily addicted prisoners to deal with their hangovers. We had a list of prisoners who needed specific medicine, and every night we dropped by their cells and made sure they took the pills. Because we had a lot of those types of pills in the health section, we transferred them to the prison sneakily. We gave them to prisoners, but because we had connections with the outside and had opportunities to import other types of drugs such as heroin, we provided ourselves with not just those pills in the health section, but also heroin. (Male participant, seven years of incarceration)

Offenders who repeatedly were imprisoned for petty crimes were assumed to have insufficient criminal skills and knowledge; thus, it was considered shameful to make friends with recidivists in prison. Recidivists lost their status in the eye of prisoners and correctional officers as well. However, if recidivists built strong connections with leaders and drug dealers, they built social capital, received more information about inmate social life, and obtained permission from leaders to import drugs each time they are incarcerated, to achieve respect and status.

Prisoners with a heavy criminal history and long-term incarceration period had a really comfortable life there because the prison was their home. In contrast, for recidivists, criminals who were incarcerated 10 times, 'their hana *did not have color anymore' (i.e., they did not have any respectful or valuable status). Most of the thieves and drug dealers were included in this category. The situations of those types of prisoners completely depended on themselves. If they made friends with a high-status prisoner and offered him a drug delivery to the prison each time they were released, they would have respect. Also, the high-status prisoner would offer him a respectful position in the prison while he was incarcerated. So, if the recidivist was brave enough to deliver drugs after each incarceration, he would have a good status in the prison. They had to be fearless to transfer drugs each time; otherwise, they had to sleep in the corridors or washrooms. We set up a goodbye party for prisoners who got released after years of incarceration, but not for recidivists who were released and then after a few weeks came back. Being incarcerated was like being on leave for them. Every few weeks or months they came back, and we asked them the question: Do you go on leave in the prison or the outside? We told them that the prison lost its honor*[2] *because of prisoners like you guys. They did not have status among us, but if they tried hard, they could find someone to talk with. However, they were considered a prisoner like others in the eyes of the guards and ward, so they could participate in classes in the prison. My friends and I did not let any prisoners like them be a member of our group. We let them be a* Shahrdar *(i.e., servant/someone who cleans the room, washes dishes and clothes, and in some cases cooks) in our cell.* (Male participant, seven years of incarceration)

Controlling the Drug Network

It is well documented that drug dealers in prison earn respect and achieve high status (Crewe 2005, 2006). Although Crewe (2005) and Mjåland (2014, 2016) related that respect and status were given by inmates toward prisoners who put their life at risk to import drugs into prison, in the current study, the most important reason behind the respect and status was that they were providing basic needs (i.e. drugs). It is important to note that not all prisoners are allowed to deal with and import drugs into prison; rather, a basis for power such as having a violent criminal history or strong connections with high-status criminals is necessary. Otherwise, drug possession would not bring power, status, or respect.

You have to fit into a certain position for importing drugs into the prison; in other words, these clothes (drugs) have to fit on your body. Someone who has drugs or delivers drugs to the prison should have a special personality or characteristics. I mean, he must be someone who others can count on, he must be a violent criminal such as a murderer, and he must be tough and serious. Otherwise, he must have connections with powerful criminals within the prison. I was a murderer, and I did not have a strong body, but the way that I behaved with others meant that nobody dared to bully me. I would say 'hi' to others reluctantly. Others told themselves that he is a murderer, how do I dare

[2] Honor is a concept rooted in the "social environment"; in other words, it relates to other people's opinions about the individuals (Oleinik 2016). The importance of honor culture in some societies is so high that it is considered an expression or correlate of human dignity.

> *to tell him something inappropriate. I was a person who could deliver drugs. Also, I had strong connections with tighdarha (violent criminals).* (Male participant, ten years of incarceration)

The status of inmates is changed by transferring drugs. Leaders (almost all of whom are drug traffickers and murderers) who are treated as gods have an exclusive right to import, distribute, and control drugs while in custody. High-status drug dealers not only have an exclusive right over drugs but also have inmates in custody.

> *I was incarcerated for more than 25 years. I transported drugs from Afghanistan to northern Iran while I was in the prison. Nobody dared to transfer drugs into this specific region of Iran. It was my territory. Yes, I was in prison, but I had constant control over drug trafficking in my city. I delivered drugs to the prison every time I was on leave, and, I had four fellows who imported drugs. There was not anybody in the prison whom I was supposed to respect, even the correctional officers; the officers, even those guys, should respect me. You know what? They did know how powerful I was. All the prisoners asked for drugs from me and if they themselves wanted to deliver drugs to the prison, they first asked me."* (Male participant, 30 years of incarceration)

> *We not only had control over drugs in the prison, but also we governed the prison through drugs. We governed the whole prison system through drugs. We were eight prisoners who had possession over all the drugs in the prison. Every two weeks, one of us went on leave and brought back drugs to the prison.* (Male participant, seven years of incarceration)

Since correctional officers showed compassion to murderers because of their being on death row, most often murderers were not inspected or searched by officers; thus, their units were the most secure and safe ones in which to store drugs. Most often, the highest-status inmates do not put their lives at risk to deliver drugs into the prison; rather, they recruited *anbari* ("storage people," mules) who carried the drugs inside their body cavity.

Most of them are untraceable, and you do not know by whom or when the drugs will be delivered to the prison. (Male participant, five years of incarceration, NA representative in the prison)

Wealth

Both drug possession and money are sources of economic capital, which creates a circle of social capital around inmates. Wealthy inmates, regardless of their criminal history and possession of drugs, attract a large amount of respect and occupy a high status in prison, since they can afford to cover all the expenses of inmates in their unit. Most participants used the idiom *Pol dashte bash koft dashte bash*, which means "have money no matter what." However, the mentioned idiom is prevalent in society as well to illustrate the importance of being rich. Money in either society or prison in Iran brings unconditional power and respect. In society, being rich means the capability to act as God and your acts are thus legitimized by default. Money plays a pivotal role in society to some extent, such that even misbehavior or law-breaking can be overlooked. Hanging out or communicating with rich inmates in the prison guarantees drug, food, respect, and safety. Inmates with no money cannot afford even their daily needs, such as food, let alone drugs. In drug-related units, new convicts with no money and no drugs must spend their very first weeks in the halls and washrooms until they find some connections and friends to support them. Most of them will work in the prison as a *shahdar* (servant). They cook food and wash dishes and clothes to receive drugs and food in return. Being a servant of other inmates is common among addicted and poor inmates in order to receive drugs regularly.

I did everything to have one gram of methamphetamine in prison. I had just entered the prison. I knew nobody, and nobody cared about new convicts. I was out of drugs and money, and I could not stand those withdrawal feelings. My body became wracked with pain, and I went crazy. I had to beg for food and drugs. One of the managers of the cells offered for me to be the servant of the cell to earn food and drugs in return. I cooked food and washed dishes every day to have one plate of food and one gram of drugs. Sometimes they did not give me drugs, they just shared their drugs with me. (Male participant, two years of incarceration)

> *The prison atmosphere is the same as the outside; if you have money you will be fine. The best beds were sold to the wealthy ones. They were not expected to wash their dishes and clothes, as someone else provided those services. Other prisoners did not let anybody in the prison give the wealthy ones a bad look or assault them. What I mean is that everybody gave special attention to the wealthy prisoners. On the contrary, everybody assaulted the poor ones, who were incapable of protecting themselves. It is enough for bullies to see slight misbehaviour from the poor prisoners; they forced them to be a servant for one month as a punishment.* (Male participant, eight years of incarceration)

Since prisoners in some sections of prison, especially the drug-related criminals' section, had to buy drugs, extra food, a bed, clothes, and cigarettes from the high-status prisoners, having money means having power, which brings respect. Prisoners prefer to communicate with someone who has money in their account, because they can afford to help them occasionally.

> *People in the prison care about you if you have money; they support you and respect you because you have money. You can buy something they could not buy. This means that if someone on the outside cares about the prisoner, then she has support. She could buy drugs for you if you wash her dishes and clothes. She could afford my life, too. Prisoners who do not have money have to wash others' clothes and dishes to have one pack of cigarettes or one plate of food. Nobody respects them.* (Female participant, five years of incarceration)

Other prisoners declared that prison can be as comfortable as a hotel if you have money in your account.

> *These days, if you have money then prison is going to be like a hotel for you. Also, you might have servants. They respect you because of your money.* (Female participant, two years of incarceration)

Spiritual Identity

Possession of either criminal identity or spiritual identity brings about the most respected and powerful positions in the penal system. As debated earlier, the contradictory social structure of prisons requires contradictory social actions and performances. While being violent and harsh in prison is valued, being honorable and high-minded (*loti*) is considered a means to maintaining superior status.

> *There are some prisoners who always act violently in the prison toward other prisoners in every situation, so most of the prisoners do what they order. But this is a temporary status, because there might be the possibility of the emergence of another prisoner who is more violent than him, so he could lose power and respect. Then, most of the prisoners will start to obey the second prisoner's commands. We had one of these types of violent prisoner who scared everyone; all other prisoners were forced to respect him and feared him. After two years of holding a dominant position, a young prisoner who was just 18 years old entered the prison and, in a fight, injured him badly with a knife. After this, nobody feared him, and nobody respected him anymore. The dominant violent status has been held by that young man ever since that day. If the prisoners do not put a limit on their violent behaviour and if they do not control themselves and if they constantly force prisoners to obey their command, they will lose respect day by day. For example, if you bully older prisoners and force them to do something against their will, you lose your respect. If you are the cause of a lot of the bullying in the prison, for sure one day someone who is crazier will come to the prison and defeat you. You have to be* loti *in the prison, which means being the hero of humanity and dignity, being half a kilo (i.e., not having much physical strength) but being a man and never a bully.* (Male participant, nine years of incarceration)

According to the interviews, there is a group of prisoners who are violent criminals but do not act as criminals in the prison; they act as mediators between inmates. They are called *rish sefid* (literally means one with a "white beard," but in fact means a man of wisdom who can solve problems by being a just mediator), and it is not a matter of age but of spiritual identity. In fact, respecting *rish sefid* is one of the exceptional occasions in which the concept of respect is not an illusion. Respecting violent criminals, wealthy prisoners, and drug possessors implies the illusion of respect, which is hidden behind basic needs. Mediators not only are problem solvers, but also, if they are wealthy enough, can afford to help with other prisoners' lives; they provide financial support for inmates.

> *At the first stage, in order to be respected by other prisoners, you have to have a violent criminal history. Also, you must behave and act violently, as if you are superior and harsh on some occasions. On the other hand, there are some who are high-minded and honorable in prison. There are some prisoners who are so young, but they are so respected. They do not force anyone to do anything; they do not order anyone around. There was a young man in the prison who was just 26 years old. He had murdered someone by shooting them 9 times, and that was one of the cruelest murders among all the prisoners. But in the prison, he was a fixer between two different groups who were constantly fighting. When he gave advice to solve the problem of the fighting, nobody declined or ignored him. All the prisoners obeyed his advice and suggestions, just because he was an honest and trustworthy man. Even the managers of the prison stood up in front of him and respected him. Even if prisoners wanted to start a fight against another group, they talked with him first. You just knew his status in the prison was stable. He always had the respect of others because of his honorable behaviour.* (Male participant, nine years of incarceration)

> *Mediators are not only there to take care of their cellmates' expenses but also, if the prison needs something, they are the first to volunteer to buy it. They even financially support their friends to protect them from selling themselves for the sake of drugs. They are wealthy, but they spend money on the prisoners. All prisoners know that he sacrificed his money and time to gain the credit and honor of others. He was the one who even had the respect of the warden.* (Male participant, eight years of incarceration)

There are some prisoners who received respect parallel to *loti* and *rish sefid* in the prison; they were called *fardin* (i.e. innocent prisoners who took responsibility for their guilty loved ones' crimes and got imprisoned on behalf of them), and they had the most respect. Additionally, some of the senior prisoners in some units (i.e. mostly on death row) are considered a source of calm and hope. Their cells act as a shrine in the prison where they can spiritually support other inmates.

> *There was an old prisoner who was a drug trafficker, incarcerated for 15 years. All prisoners respected him because he prayed for all of us and kept us calm and gave us hope.* (Male participant, three years of incarceration)

> *When I was released, all the prisoners were happy for me because I read the Quran for them to help them relax. I was a storyteller. They all respected me.* (Female participant, two years of incarceration)

Social Capital

Most violent criminals have been excluded by their family members since they were imprisoned. Even those who were drug addicts and were incarcerated for possessing a small amount of drugs did not receive any attention from their families.

> *The reality is that every day in the prison we were faced with being ignored by our family members outside the prison. They did not care about us. Whenever I called them, they immediately started to yell at me and verbally assault me. They did not help me to endure the prison circumstances. I asked them several times to make a pledge to set me free for a while, but they ignored it all the time. So, in this situation where we were not important for anybody around us, the only thing that can ease the pressure is to take drugs. We use drugs to release all our emotional pain.* (Male participant, three years of incarceration)

In addition to the social, political, cultural, and economic impacts of society on the inmates' social world, the impact of family support, both emotional and financial, is undeniable. Inmates who have visits, phone calls, and letters from their families have higher status and respect than others. Having constant contact with the outside world implies that the inmate has enough money to buy drugs and food. Also, it illustrates that the inmate still has the emotional support of family members and has not been excluded from his/her small community, even if he/she has already been excluded by society. Having respect and status among family members and loved ones directly affects the status of a prisoner among others and even among the staff. Most of the incarcerated men considered family support as a credit, which is an automatic bonus in terms of prestige.

> *Prisoners who do not have visitors earn no respect in the prison because subsequently they do not have any deposits.* (Male participant, four years of incarceration)

The domino effect of exclusion from family, friends, and society has become an ordinary fact among incarcerated women, and while it impacts their behaviors, emotions, and feelings inside prison, it does not have even a slight effect on women's status in prison. Accepting the reality that they are the forgotten members of their family and being treated as socially and emotionally "dead bodies" can justify why family support is not considered as important among incarcerated men. Being excluded from the family and then the society is a preordained fact in incarcerated women's minds. They have known that every slight misbehavior might jeopardize their families' honor and subsequently push them into the isolation zone. According to the interviews, some of the addicted women had a temporary marriage with addicted men or drug dealers and had children and were also the breadwinners of their family. Because of this dishonorable behavior, they do not expect their family to support them emotionally or financially while they are incarcerated. Their family excluded them during their addiction.

> *Once my family found out that I was addicted to heroin, my father kicked me out of the home. I could not come back to see my family, because every time my father saw me around, he beat me so hard. He told me that I was the shame of the family. I was in the prison for five years, and I did not see my siblings in that time. After three years of begging her to visit me, my mother came to see me. My family did not even deposit money in my account. I did not have money to buy anything. It does not matter; I had been used to this kind of behaviour since I was 11. Since my father saw a cigarette in my hand, the exclusions and assaults started. They did not care about me, ever; I did not exist. How could I expect them to help now? What can they say to the family? When I got incarcerated, I was pregnant, and my family did not know. After two years, they found out that I was pregnant. Then, my mother called me and told me that if you tell any members of the family that you have a child, you will never ever see us again. I was an addict, I was a murderer, I got temporarily married to a drug dealer, and I got incarcerated. How can I expect them to visit me?* (Female participant, eight years of incarceration)

Several studies have been done regarding the interactions of incarcerated mothers and children both inside and outside of prisons around the world (Fritsch and Burkhead 1981; Poehlmann 2005; Eddy and Reid 2002; Hissel et al. 2011; Foster and Hagan 2007; Hungerford 1993; Johnson 2009; Johnson and Waldfogel 2002; Murray et al. 2009; Scharff-Smith and Gampell 2011; DeFina and Hannon 2010). The only visitors that some women expect to have are their children; most often, incarcerated women are mothers of children and inseparable relationships between them are a usual and acceptable fact among women, though they do not receive any credit for them. Being in constant connection with the outside world, especially with children, decreases the pain of isolation and frustration. According to Anaraki and Boostani (2014, p. 2452), "The child's presence beside the mother made them calm, even sometimes helped them to fight the anxiety of bad events." It is important to consider that the only group of imprisoned women who were not involved in drug economies or power struggles in the inmates' social world were incarcerated mothers. Almost all of them had serious drug addictions, while incarceration either along with their children or while separated from them was a final push for them to change their lifestyle. Incarcerated mothers were locked up in separate units with their children, and there was no trace of drugs there. However, the most long-term, violent criminal among the mothers was assigned to manage the unit. All mothers started the process of drug withdrawal in the prison, since they felt guilty about leaving their children on the other side of the wall or having their children be part of the inmate world. The mothers' unit was exempt from all kinds of violence, social disorders, misbehavior, and disobedience. The mothers' unit was less affected by instability as a result of changing leaders and social orders in prison. Mothers are not considered criminals in prison. Contrary to the feelings of society on the other side of the walls, their identity as a mother was the most salient among the multiple identities used to label female drug addicts in society. An incarcerated mother with her child has a respectful status in the prison, but this does not necessarily bring power and authority. I will return to the situation of incarcerated women with children in prison in Chap. 4.

> *My children were the only visitors that I had. They came to see me despite all their financial issues. They missed me, especially when they found out that I am sentenced to death. They came to see me every month. Can you believe that they do not have anyone to support them? They themselves work hard to afford their lives, and they even send me money. They are my only source of calmness, the only way that I can survive this circumstance.* (Female participant, six years of incarceration)

> *I play with my kid all day and night and speak to him lovingly. I devote all my time to my kid.* (Incarcerated mother, five years of incarceration, on death row)

> *I really have fun with my son Hussein. We all care for our babies, wash their clothes, feed them, cuddle them as they return from kindergarten and play with them.* (Incarcerated mother, three years of incarceration, on death row)

Along with the influences of the outside world on prisoners' lives inside the prison, having social capital and social ties inside the prison are both means of gaining high status and respect.

> *I did not make a friend when I was imprisoned the first time, but in the next times, I made a lot of friends. I found that some of the prisoners have their relatives there. For example, one of them who had her mother in the prison was a manager of one of the cells. So, they found that having a bed in the prison is easier than having no friends and relatives. I got to know some of the prisoners during different incarcerations. I got to know my friend's mom, and she introduced me to the manager of health care. Thus, the incarceration got easier and easier over time. I made friends with my friend's mom in the prison. It was not possible to make friends with others in prison while you are just a poor addict. The only way is to have some connection outside of the prison which gives you the opportunity to make a friend with someone. Anyway, my friend's mom worked in the health care centre in the prison, and whenever I needed painkillers, she immediately gave me one. During my first incarceration, I had so much pain because I did not have drugs. I asked for painkillers but because I did not know anybody in the health care centre, and I did not get even one painkiller to ease my pain. My situation in prison during the second and third time of incarceration was better than the first time, because I found several friends.* (Female participant, two years of incarceration)

Social capital also plays a pivotal role in changing the status of people who use drugs in compulsory camps. Most of the addicts in compulsory camps were arrested on the street, since almost all of them were homeless. Although there are night drop-in centers for homeless sex workers and people who use drugs, especially in Tehran, most of them spend their lives on the street. Those who have a family who can reach out to them in the compulsory camps received more respect. This is not because of the money that he/she might receive from the family while locked up in the camps; rather, the emotional support they receive is vital. Since most homeless drug addicts have been separated from their family intentionally or unintentionally, they suffer from not being supported by them. Most of them have not seen their family members in ten years. One of the addict women in the night drop-in center in Tehran spent her life in South Tehran with only a bicycle. Her family forced her to leave home 11 years ago, and since then, they have never let her back, even to see her siblings. Her life revolved around riding her bicycle;[3] she was arrested by the police and sent to compulsory camps more than three times. Each time she had to leave her bicycle somewhere in the street and get into the police car. She spent most nights in the treatment centers, except those nights she spent in the compulsory camps. She came to the center regularly at 7 p.m. and started by washing her clothes and bicycle and taking a shower. She states:

> *I used to be arrested and sent for a drug test and then moved to the compulsory camps. The camps are all like prison but even worse. At least in the prison there are some rules and red lines that nobody dares to cross. But in the camps, there is nothing to control addicts but beating, beating, and beating. All of them were sent there to quit drugs compulsorily, and most of them count down to the day to their release when they can start using drugs again. In this situation, if you have someone who can take care of you or at least have regular visits with family members, this changes everything for you. All other addicts in the camps are jealous of those who have someone who loves them or at least is willing to help them. (Female participant, three years of incarceration)*

[3] Women riding a bike in Iran is a delinquent act in itself; in 2016, Supreme Leader, Ayatollah Ali Khamenei "appeared to crush the notion with a fatwa explicitly banning women from cycling in public, but it was not strictly enforced" (Bezhan 2019). https://www.rferl.org/a/iran-women-banned-cycling-isfahan/29949683.html.

Sexuality

It is well documented that homosexuality is a pervasive phenomenon in prisons across the world, and there have been several studies of homosexuality in prison (Hensley 2000; Lockwood 1980; Wooden and Parker 1982; Nacci and Kane 1984; Richmond 1978; Saum et al. 1995; Struckman-Johnson et al. 1996; Tewksbury 1989). However, there is a lack of literature about homosexuality in the penal world of Iran. Since homophobia is pervasive in the Iranian society (Khoshnood et al. 2008), negative beliefs, values, and ideas are imported into prison as well. Homosexual activity in the Islamic Republic of Iran is punishable by imprisonment, lashes, and execution based on the Islamic penal code.[4] According to interviews, having sexual activity in prison is the most

[4] According to the Islamic Penal code: Article 233, "*Livat* is defined as penetration of a man's sex organ (penis), up to the point of circumcision, into another male person's anus. "Article 234, "The *hadd* punishment for *livat* shall be the death penalty for the insertive/active party if he has committed *livat* by using force, coercion, or in cases where he meets the conditions for *ihsan*; otherwise, he shall be sentenced to one hundred lashes. The *hadd* punishment for the receptive/passive party, in any case (whether or not he meets the conditions for *ihsan*) shall be the death penalty." Note 2: "*Ihsan* is defined as a status that a man is married to a permanent and pubescent wife and whilst he has been sane and pubescent has had a vaginal intercourse with the same wife while she was pubescent, and he can have an intercourse with her in the same way [vaginal] whenever he so wishes." Article 235, "*Tafkhiz* is defined as putting a man's sex organ (penis) between the thighs or buttocks of another male person. Note: A penetration [of a penis into another male person's anus] that does not reach the point of circumcision shall be regarded as *tafkhiz*." Article 236, in the case of *tafkhiz*, the *hadd* punishment for the active and passive party shall be one hundred lashes and it shall make no difference whether or not the offender meets the conditions of *ihsan* [mentioned in note 2 of Article 234], or whether or not [the offender] has resorted to coercion." "Note: If the active party is a non-Muslim and the passive party is a Muslim, the *hadd* punishment for the active party shall be the death penalty." Article 237, "Homosexual acts of a male person in cases other than *livat* and *tafkhiz*, such as kissing or touching as a result of lust, shall be punishable by thirty-one to seventy-four lashes of *ta'zir* punishment of the sixth grade." "Note 1: This article shall be equally applicable in the case of a female person. Note 2: This article shall not be applicable in the cases punishable by a *hadd* punishment under *Shari'a* rules." Article 238, "*Musaheqeh* is defined as where a female person puts her sex organ on the sex organ of another person of the same sex." Article 239, "The *hadd* punishment for *musaheqeh* shall be one hundred lashes." Article 240, "Regarding the *hadd* punishment for *musaheqeh*, there is no difference between the active or passive parties or between Muslims and non-Muslims, or between a person who meets the conditions for *ihsan* and a person who does not, and also whether or not [the offender] has resorted to coercion."

shameful act, resulting in the offenders having the lowest of the low statuses allocated to them.

Most often, homosexual relationships begin by just accepting a powerful inmate's offer of food, bed, drugs, and protection. Most first-time inmates who accept those offers and accept being taken under their wing are surprised that they are expected to be a sexual partner in return. The inmates who accept having a passive (inferior) position in a sexual relationship are a principal target of stigma, while the active (superior) one is less affected by inmates' views.

> *You may find a lot of prisoners in the washroom from late at night to the morning who have used drugs or had sexual relations.* (Male participant, five years of incarceration)

> *Homosexuality is a pervasive phenomenon in prisons, and homosexuals do not have the respect of other prisoners. They sell their bodies. They do not have any status in the prison. Their status is even less than that of a servant who works for other prisoners in order to buy drugs and food. We called them* Arbab to Delly. *They sell their bodies for the sake of drugs. They are trash.* (Male participant, five years of incarceration)

Also, many inmates do not have conjugal visits (i.e. a type of visiting that is specified for married couples); consequently, they felt frustrated and overwhelmed in prison. As one participant declared: "*the only escapes for them are drugs, gambling, and sex.*" These are most often high-status criminals, who intend to have situational sexual relations with the intention of filling the deprivation they experience. However, most of the prisoners (in a passive or inferior position) who get involved in sexual activities simply need financial assistance.

> *It is much better to beg for drugs and food than to be a sexual partner in prison.* (Male participant, four years of incarceration)

> *Although a* shahdar *does not have any respect and status in the prison, they at least have dignity in comparison with those who sell themselves in return for food and drugs.* (Male participant, seven years of incarceration)

> *Some prisoners who did not have financial support decided to wash others' clothes and dishes to earn money. But some others preferred to be a sexual partner of someone to be financially provided for. Although nobody dares to get close to him because of his owner or boss, he did not have respect in prison, and he lost his status immediately.* (Male participant, five years of incarceration)

There is a deeper stigma attached to homosexual activity among incarcerated women; they are called *golo goldon* (flower and pot). Although some studies report a less homophobic reaction to female homosexuality either in prison or society at large (see Hensley 1995, 2000; Herek 1988; Kurdek 1988; LaMar and Kite 1998; Price and Dalecki 1998; Seltzer 1992; Sigelman et al. 1991; Van de Ven 1994; Kite and Whitley 1996; Herek and Capitanio 1999; Plugge-Foust and Strickland 2000; Giallombardo 1966; Koscheski and Hensley 2001; Ward and Kassebaum 1964), incarcerated women feel more negatively toward homosexual activity than men, and there are also strict unwritten rules applied as deterrents in women's prisons (i.e. incarcerated women are not allowed to wear makeup, change clothes in public, whisper with other inmates, put their head on their friend's shoulder, take their friend's hand, or write letters to other inmates). Incarcerated women in this study deployed two strategies in Iranian prisons to cope with separation from their family: pseudo families (will be discussed in a section related to gangs in prison) and homosexual relations. Most interviewees declared that homosexual activity among incarcerated women is used as an attempt to meet emotional needs. However, any sexual "deviance" will be stigmatized and punished by correctional officers (e.g. losing jobs, cleaning washrooms for one week, losing respect of the officers) and inmates (e.g. inmates start to spread rumors to drag her down from a high-status position). It is the best means in the hands of the enemy to take the power away from prisoners who have had positive influences on correctional officers and have been allocated a good position. The social and psychological pressure of stigmatization because of sexual activity acts as a fatal poison, targeting the status of inmates. In Iranian prisons all women are required to wear hijab; if they refuse to do so they will be punished extremely.[5]

> *In the women's prison, we could not build a close relationship with each other, because once you start a close relationship with someone else in the prison, other prisoners make rumors about you having a sexual relationship with her. The sexual stigma is something usual in women's prisons. Taking someone's hand and putting your head on someone's shoulder are forbidden, because once you do that rumors are started, and guards become suspicious. I wrote a letter for one of my friends in the prison, and someone found out and gave it to the guards. Since then, there have been a lot of rumors about me, and my story became one of the most important topics there. I cried several times because of the rumors. The punishments for any possible and potential homosexual behaviour included getting fired from my job, cutting off in-person visiting, and cutting off telephone coupons. If you are the favorite ones of the guards, they give you the option to choose your punishment, and if you do not choose anything, they tell you that you are a rebel and harshly punish you. I remember that I chose cleaning the bathrooms for one week. Guards told me, "You have to clean them as a reminder that you are in prison even though you hold a high position." All prisoners tried to hide their relationships in the prison. They punished me for writing a letter to a girl. In fact, homosexuality in the women's prison was limited by the control of emotional expression. Therefore, talking sexy and writing letters were forbidden. Some of the homosexual prisoners even continued their relations after being released, and they moved out together. The homosexual stigma does not just affect prisoners; guards are another target for this type of stigma. Some of the guards and employees in the prison are so cautious about what prisoners think and say about them, and it is important for them to protect their honor and dignity in the prison. Although we are all women in the prison, you are not allowed to change your clothes in front of others.* (Female participant, five years of incarceration)

[5] As one of the homosexual participants said: *"I was punished from the first day that I was incarcerated. I was arrested because of not wearing a hijab in the street, and the police officers who arrested me knew me well, since I hung out with boys and used drugs in the park. One day, they told me, 'If we see you around one more time without a hijab, you will be arrested'. They arrested me and now that I am in a prison with all women, they force me to wear a hijab. I refuse each time, and I am punished. I am not a woman. I do not like to wear a hijab. It is ridiculous."*

Loyalty

According to interviewees, the status of *mokhber* (snitch/informant), those who were assigned by correctional officers to report on others, was not even equivalent to the status of inmates who were situationally homosexual in order to afford their life inside prison. The importance of information in prison is so great that all prisoners are advised on the very first days of incarceration that secrecy is paramount; also, it is one of the most important indicators of loyalty in the inmates' social world.

> *On the first day that I entered the prison, the boss of the cell told me in private that whatever you see you have to keep it to yourself. If you see a half kilogram of drugs anywhere in this prison, you should not tell anybody about it. You must keep everything to yourself. If any prisoners talk, they will be excluded and thrown out of the cell. If a prisoner gets close to the warden, even if they have known each other from childhood, he will be considered a snitch. It is even worse than being a sexual partner of someone in the prison.* (Male participant, ten years of incarceration)

The punishments for being *mokhber* ranged from being excluded from the prison society to being killed by cellmates.

> *Snitches are dead bodies. Their corpses will move out of the prison; we will burn them with hot water.* (Male participant, five years of incarceration)

The former punishment is more torturous than the latter; in other words, prisoners who have been already excluded and isolated in the society and rarely have visits with their families will be excluded again in this last-chance society, the so-called total institution.

> *Nobody in the prison wants to be a cellmate with a snitch. When prisoners learned that somebody is a snitch in the cell, they do not even talk in front of him. We will do everything to force him to leave the cell and stay in the yard the whole day. Nobody talks to him; he is like a ghost. His circumstances will be the worst if he discloses information and gets somebody in trouble. We will not let him stay in the cell for one more second; he must leave. If he was lucky enough*

to not be killed, he will be alone in the prison. (Male participant, eight years of incarceration)

Some snitches are not only psychologically punished (i.e. being excluded and exposed to humiliating jokes), they are physically tortured as well. Drug networks in women's prisons are as serious and complicated as in men's prisons; the whole process of trafficking, dealing, selling, and using drugs in prison is considered high-security information. Since drugs are deemed a basic need in prison society, disclosing information regarding drugs is punishable by death.

One of the inmates leaked information about the usage of methamphetamine in his cell, so his cellmates poured hot sauce in his anus and kicked him out of the cell. We accepted him in our cell, but we made jokes about the hot sauce and always laughed at him. (Male participant, three years of incarceration)

Making rumors and disclosing information is a usual phenomenon in women's prison. One of the most important tools in the hands of women in prison is generating rumors; instead of using physical violence against each other, they cause mental torture. Although disclosing information is common among incarcerated women, most often this information involves the stigma of homosexuality.

Captives as a Society

Although various studies have discussed deprivation as a common characteristic of prisons around the world, this was not the case for leaders in Iranian prisons. Violent criminals, especially drug traffickers, have adequate facilities and private spaces to create a palace at the heart of the prison, so they were called "kings of prison." Although transparency and exposure to the prison public do not allow prisoners to have a private space, prisoners are all advised not to look in any cells or any beds other than their own, and, to be open about their crimes.

All prisoners, without exception, have to be clear about their crimes, because whether they are or not, all prisoners will be informed.(Male participant, nine years of incarceration)

We fight because of petty issues. Someone entered our cell without our permission, so I threw a bottle toward his head. (Male participant, three years of incarceration)

Also, some cells have their own private place between the beds for using drugs; they called them *dakhme* (cellar). The peaceful coexistence of privacy and transparency in the prison causes a constant internal war for prisoners; contradictory to social actions in the prison, this acts as a barrier to the emergence of the unit-based identity in prison.

Having privacy in a highly transparent institution requires a criminal history, economic capital, and social capital within the penal world. Being a professional and wealthy drug trafficker has enormous financial benefits for both prisoners and correctional officers. The reality of having the authority to build a palace in the prison is hidden under the cover of respect; this is nothing but a basic need. Those types of prisoners, of whom there are only one or two in each prison, are considered kings not only in the prison territory but also in the drug community within the society. Incarcerating powerful drug traffickers not only expands their networks from society to the prison, which is the place with highest demand for drugs, but also brings financial benefits for correctional officers as well. According to one of the participants who had about 30 years of incarceration in all parts of Iran and had been one of the most important drug traffickers for almost 20 years in the region from Afghanistan to north of Iran:

I did not eat regular food in the prison; I ordered food and some of my friends brought my orders to the prison for me. The bars of my cell were always closed and were covered with a curtain. That was not usual in the prison. Nobody was allowed to cover their door with a curtain; they could not even cover their own beds with anything. Everything had to be as transparent as possible. Everybody is a witness to all your activities. However, that did not apply to prisoners like me. I remember one time when I got incarcerated, the correctional officers knew me well. I was notified that they wanted to come to arrest me, so I did not escape. I stayed in my house in the jungle and waited for them. When they came, I told them that I had to bring my private belongings into the prison. I was incarcerated in solitary confinement for one month with all my private belongings. They all knew me; whenever I was incarcerated, they knew that a large amount of drugs would be transferred to the prison without a doubt. I ignored the prison's rules, but I made friends with the guards. Although they knew that by incarcerating me nothing was going to happen in the society, they still incarcerated me. Some of them were very cooperative with me when it came to delivering drugs. (Male participant, thirteen years of incarceration)

Kings of prison recruit young low-status inmates like a kind of prison "minions" (*noche)* to provide security information about inmates and correctional officers. The subculture of *noche parvari* (*noche* refers to a novice young man as a petty servant) is a pervasive phenomenon in inmate society. They have a subordinate position; however, in return for disclosing information, their boss provides them with the best-quality drugs, food, and beds. It can be said that *noche* exists in a reciprocal relationship between the powerful criminals and the subordinate inmates; the status of powerful prisoners is guaranteed through not only their criminal history, money, and drug possession, but also through their *noche,* who increases the knowledge of their boss by snitching everywhere in the prison; vulnerable inmates are protected from victimization under the protection of their boss. Despite all advice regarding the importance of keeping information confidential and not acting as a snitch in prison, being a snitch for powerful prisoners does not have the same consequences as being the snitch of correctional officers. Every single prisoner knows who the *noche* is, and that they are protected by the most powerful leader in the prison.

Prisoners such as myself who are wealthy and take charge of drug trafficking in the prison have 7 or 8 noche around us. I had a noche outside of the prison as well. In the prison, they updated me with fresh news about events that had happened in the prison. They notified me of whatever they had seen or heard that might affect my position in the prison. I did not give them money. I had a handkerchief that was soaked with heroin. I brought that into the prison; that handkerchief was drenched with a half kilogram of heroin. In return for protecting my powerful status in the prison by snitching and flattering, I gave them a small part of my handkerchief. I provided them with good-quality food and a bed in the prison and even helped them outside of the prison when they got released. (Male participant, 30 years of incarceration)

High-status criminals (kings) are the only exceptional groups in the prison who are not affected by homosexual stigma. Likewise, there are reciprocal relationships between the boss (*arbab*) and the servant (*noche*), where the sexual partners support their bosses (owners) emotionally and physically and receive food, drugs, and a bed in return. The low-status inmates who are sexual partners of the high-status ones must tolerate all the weight of stigma in prison. Meanwhile, homosexual activities among the high-status prisoners are not only considered as having no shame or dishonor but are also considered a sign of power. High-status inmates, when involved in homosexual relationships, play, as a rule, an active role, whereas a passive role is reserved to their sexual partners. A high status in prison, similarly to a high status in all masculine cultures, is associated with playing an active role in sexual act.

High-status criminals in women's prisons have sexual partners as well, and this is not a stigma, nor even a source of shame for them. Those who are being spied on or being stigmatized are low-status prisoners. The stigma of homosexuality can drag all types of prisoners down but not the high-status violent criminals who have control over almost all activities in prison.

> *Some of the leaders in prison, who have always been violent criminals, have sexual partners, but no one would dare to report any of their homosexual activities in the prison. They are violent criminals with long-term experiences in the prison. They are proud of having sexual partners.* (Female participant, two years of incarceration)

Homosexual relations in the inmate world do not always involve physical contact; high-status inmates who do not have any physical contact with their sexual partners, just companionship with them for comfort, are called *rokh baz* (someone who enjoys a beautiful face) or *mashami* (someone who enjoys good-smelling and good-looking people).

> *When the cell's boss takes a beautiful prisoner under his wing, it means that he belongs to him. Most of them are* rokh baz, *who do not touch their partners; it just feels sexy to communicate with these beautiful guys. When they cannot have*

intercourse, they use their eyes. Just by looking and smelling they gain sexual satisfaction. (Male participant, four years of incarceration)

He just gave me a bed and as much as food as I wanted. He gave me the bed closest to himself. He hired someone to wash my clothes. I did not do anything. He enjoyed my company. He did not let me do anything. I did not know what he wanted. Once I came to the prison, he chose me and told me that I had to stay by his side. (Male participant, seven months of incarceration).

Battle Zone

Most of the fighting and physical violence circulates around three factors: drug, sex, and safety. Since drugs play a pivotal role in enduring and surviving the time behind bars, any slight disorder in the process of drug distribution is intolerable. Methadone was systematically delivered to inmates by the health department, which decreased any possible risk of violence as a result of prisoners suffering withdrawal. Methadone is the most common form of medication-assisted treatment in prison, which consists of a daily dose prescription and cost approximately $7 per month in 2017. Methadone therapy was not only cost effective but also the best treatment for heroin dependence; however, most of the prisoners claimed that not only did they use methadone, but other drugs available in the prison as well. In fact, the official policy of distributing methadone across prisons aims at two goals: treating addiction and decreasing violence in the prison. The first goal has not been achieved at all due to the high dependency on methadone as an alternative drug and the availability of other drugs in prison. However, the monitoring and controlling of prisoners through the methadone treatments was an undeniable fact. By paying just $7 monthly, some prisoners were able to receive a certain amount of methadone. Thus, every morning the prison physician distributed methadone at different doses for different prisoners based on their drug abuse history. However, even though different efforts have been made to reduce drug-related violence in prison, it is still the hidden reason behind much of the fighting.

Most fights in prison happen because of drugs; for the 3 months that I was incarcerated in prison, I fought around 40 times over drugs. I remember one day when drugs were prohibited in the prison, prisoners set up a protest to fight and beat guards, forcing them to make drugs available. Drugs are like oxygen for us in the prison. Any slight move against drug use will face an extreme reaction from the prisoners. Nobody in the cell dares to protest against other inmates using drugs in the cell, or they will be beaten so hard. (Male participant, ten years of incarceration)

Without the slightest doubt, most of the fights in the prison are due to drugs. About 80% of fighting centres around drugs. The rest (20%) concerns prisoners who are aggressive and violent. For example, they knife you if you just look at them in a way they do not like. (Male participant, two years of incarceration)

I was in the Kanon *(a separate section in prison for youth) for 6 months. When turned 18 years old, I was moved to the central prison. One of the biggest and most violent rebellions I had ever seen in the prison happened in the Kanon. The rebellion started from a small fight between two friends because of drugs, and suddenly about 100 prisoners started to fight. The chaos was so bad that the guards ran away. The prisoners exploded all the fire extinguishers. At last, at midnight, two buses full of guards with tear gas (lachrymators) invaded the prison. Beforehand, the ward of the prison with the Quran in his hand came to the prison and told us 'I swear on the Quran I will not do anything if you let me in.' We let him in, and he just moved the main perpetrators of the disaster, and we did not see them again.* (Male participant, seven years of incarceration)

According to Article 42 of the Anti-Narcotic Law of the Islamic Republic of Iran, "the Judicature power is permitted to maintain some of the drug-related convicts in special camps (with tight or normal conditions) rather than prisons. The government has a duty to provide necessary funds, facilities and regulations for managing such camps in a period of one year." Thus, keeping with this strategy, two compulsory labor camps (*Asad Abad*) were established in Isfahan to house drug-related offenders in separate prisons. According to interviewees, those labor camps were the most chaotic prisons; all prisoners in this section were people who use drugs with no exception, being arrested directly for drug offences. Violence is a prevalent phenomenon in labor camps. Being surrounded with drug users and drug dealers, there was increased availability of all kinds of drugs at affordable prices (i.e. cheaper than in any other types of prisons), and the rate of death resulting from drug overdose was extremely high. These camps were nothing more than a locked-up space for drug users in a chaotic world. An interviewee described how drug users were employed in labor camps (*Asad Abad*); however, the minimum wage was CAD 10, so most inmates refused to work. The privileges of working in factories located in prisons included free calls and visit opportunities with family. Those inmates in labor camps who chose to work gradually stole the factories' products and created a black market to sell them in prison.

> *The drug-related units in the prison were the most dangerous and unsafe parts of the prison. To punish prisoners in other sections, especially murderers, they would exile them to the drug section. There were continued fights among prisoners who could not be controlled at all. Even with methadone being distributed every day, there are several prisoners who need other drugs as well. Some of them did not have money, and they would do anything to get drugs. If one group of prisoners found out about the existence of drugs in another cell, they would fight to take their drugs.* (Male participant, three years of incarceration)

> *I was in* Asad Abad, *which was established for drug-related offenders. Actually, I wanted to escape from that prison because it was unbearable. I went to sleep one night, and in the morning, my cellmate next to me had passed away; he had overdosed. It was difficult to see someone pass away next to you because of drugs. There were a wide variety of drugs in that prison, and the price was not as high as in other prisons. For example, if drugs were 100,000 toman*[6] *in* Asad Abad, *they cost 300,000 toman*[7] *in the central prison of Isfahan. The opportunity for using drugs in* Asad Abad *was more than in the central prison. Although it was a fact that all kinds of offenders, from murderers to drug traffickers, were incarcerated in the central prison, and they had to deal with violent criminals, in the* Asad Abad *prison several people were murdered because of drugs. Therefore, there was no difference between these two prisons. Most of the prisoners in the* Asad Abad *prison would even prefer to be in the central prison.* (Male participant, five years of incarceration)

---

[6] US$2.

[7] US$7.

Most male participants described being involved in acts of violence several times while incarcerated; however, women declared that they did not witness violent fights in the prison. Even though they were not the potential subject of a violent act in the prison, they tried to be silent and obedient as much as they could to avoid any possible danger. While physical violence is the most common strategy used among incarcerated men, verbal violence is more common among incarcerated women.

> *I do not want to say that we did not fight or beat each other, but most often we were just insulting and making up rumors about each other.* (Female participant, five years of incarceration)

> *There were some rumors that some prisoners knifed someone to death, but we did not see or experience anything ourselves. We feared those prisoners, so we did everything that they wanted. We avoided any kind of fighting.* (Female participant, three years of incarceration)

According to interviewees, sexual partners of high-status criminals were treated as their personal property. Invading the privacy of leaders is equivalent to causing a brutal fight in prison. As a result of the prevalence of physical violence and the importance of protecting property among incarcerated men, they are more cautious than women about the sexual partners of violent criminals. Although physical violence is rare, and homosexuality is the most concealed taboo among incarcerated women, a sexual partner is the subject of much fighting in men's prison.

> *A lot of fights happened in the prison over sexual partners. Sometimes high-status prisoners broke up with one partner in favour of another, so they fought with each other. If the sexual partner had secret relationships with another prisoner, then it could lead to a huge fight. My cellmate fought 6 or 7 times during one week because of her nephew who was deemed attractive by other prisoners. Most of the time she just yelled in the yard and assaulted them verbally, but on rare occasions she beat them to ensure the safety of her nephew.* (Female participant, eight years of incarceration)

To obtain a certain degree of safety in the inmate world, fighting is unavoidable. However, prisoners' safety is always in jeopardy, and they always fear to lose it. Conditional safety has forced prisoners to fight to guarantee their safety. In two conditions, they must choose fighting over acting peacefully: (1) In the case of being assaulted, beaten, or bullied by other prisoners; and (2) If friends or cellmates are in danger. To stop any possible aggression in the future, fighting is the first preventative step. Also, to maintain their social capital, to be able to socialize with inmates, and to avoid humiliating labels such as *lashi* or *shefteyi* (e.g. coward or unworthy), prisoners must support their cellmates by fighting when required. Moreover, fighting for cellmates, friends, or gang members is a requirement for keeping one's *lati* (i.e. identity, characterized by toughness, masculinity, violence, aggressiveness) in prison.

> *You have to fight with someone who did something wrong to you; otherwise, he will misuse you constantly.* (Male participant, nine years of incarceration)

> *If you fight to support your friends, next time that you are incarcerated, all of your ex-cellmates will support you and give you a bed and food.* (Male participant, three years of incarceration)

It is worth noting that violence is a constant presence in the compulsory camps. Using violence is seen as the best strategy to control people who use drugs, as most of them are not ready to quit abusing drugs yet. In fact, most of them have not even committed any crime, and did not even possess drugs at the time of arrest. In the name of the "purification plan" (*tarh-e paksazi*), anti-narcotic police officers arrest all those whose appearance or behavior seems suspicious. One might even be with one's children, but this would not deter the police to stop and interrogate on grounds of drug suspicion. One of the female addicts who had several experiences in compulsory camps and prisons stated:

> *From the beginning to the end of the process, we are victims of severe violence beyond your imagination. Police enforcers, in front of everybody on the street, forced us to get into their car. They did not even pay attention to my four-year-old girl. The last time I was arrested on the street, I was with her. Can you imagine that they did not even look at my child? She cried and shouted in street until one of my friends in the night drop-in centre saw us and came to pick her*

up from the street. If you show resistance to getting in the car, you will be beaten hard and assaulted. When they transferred us to the camp, we had to wait in a line for a drug test, and if it was positive, the misery began. There is no soft language over there. You must listen to the personnel, or you will be beaten. The answer to even slightly bad behaviour is violence. You know why? Because none of the addicts there want to quit drugs. They break glass and throw everything. The personnel are forced to calm them down by threatening them or beating them. (Femal participant, two years of incarceration)

Hegemony of Drug-Related Networks

Although the pain of imprisonment and the pre-prison life trajectories of prisoners have a direct impact on the emergence of an inmate code and informal social order in custody, the subculture of prison in Iran is affected to a great extent by the hegemony of the drug network. Prison staff have declared that most prisoners with serious drug problems maintain their drug habits in prison, encouraging others to follow them. Using drugs is considered a means of acceptance into the prison community for most prisoners (i.e. to be eligible to socialize with other inmates in their gatherings). Moreover, most incarcerated drug addicts had habitually used drugs before incarceration to rid themselves of their anxiety and depression, a phenomenon called "self-medication" by Mjåland (2016). Although addiction to drugs is considered an important problem and an expected behavior, prison circumstances (e.g. availability and prevalence) have a crucial effect on the extent of drug abuse. There is a wealth of literature regarding the prevalence and availability of drugs in prisons (e.g. European Monitoring Centre for Drugs and Drug Addiction 2012; Friestad and Hansen 2005; Stover and Weilandt 2007; Strang et al. 2006; Bullock 2003; Plugge et al. 2009; Hucklesby and Wilkinson 2001; Edgar and O'Donnell 1998). Interviews with drug users, officers, consultants, and recovering addicts revealed that the availability of drugs in Iranian prisons is a controversial phenomenon.

There were unwritten rules in the prison, and whether you like it or not, whether it is your preference or not, you have to accept and practice them. Drug abuse was a pervasive phenomenon in prison, and if you did not use drugs, you

> *would undoubtedly be excluded. Imagine that from 10,000 prisoners, 9,900 prisoners used drugs. I was in a cell with 12 cellmates, all of whom were addicts, and I had to use drugs to be a part of them. I had to live a life there for however many years; it was my home.* (Male participant, ten years of incarceration)

> *When I entered the central prison, I was just 18 years old. I had to smoke something in the prison, because it was so inappropriate not to smoke. Because I was a murderer, I had committed a violent crime, and everybody respected me. If I did not smoke drugs in the prison, other prisoners would call me a 'pasteurized murderer' (a murderer who was too naïve and unprofessional to commit a murder). I did everything that was possible in the prison because of the atmosphere. Yes, I started to use drugs.* (Male participant, six years of incarceration)

When drugs are imported into the prison system through different channels, the dealing process, which involves a complex network and business, would begin. The highest-status drug dealers recruit inmates to sell and deliver drugs in different units. As I mentioned earlier, drugs in Iranian prisons become ten times more expensive than their usual price in the outside world. Inside prison, a "patch" of heroin, which is enough for one-night's use for one person, costs the equivalent of approximately CAD 70 in 2017. Most of the time, because of a lack of cash, buyers provided dealers with available and necessary products such as phone cards, food, and clothes. Some inmates asked for money from their family and friends outside to be transferred directly to a specific account provided by the dealers inside the prison. However, some inmates cannot finance their consumption even by trading their personal property, and they fall into two categories: (1) Stealing from and bullying other prisoners, and (2) Accepting to be a servant or a passive sexual partner of high-status prisoners.

One side of the coin is that professional dealers are taking advantage of the profitable drug business in the prison; however, it is not merely a matter of money that is turning the wheels of this drug trade. Rather, the point is that drug users become dependent upon the providers as the only hope for meeting a crucial need (i.e. drugs). This dependency provides an opportunity for drug providers to expand their power and influence over inmates. As was indicated earlier, possessors of drugs have power and high status, which results in receiving more respect. As Crewe (2005, p. 470) states, "power and respect are frequently conflated." All inmates, whether drug users or not, are drawn into this network and market of drugs. As interviewees repeatedly testified, 90% of inmates in each cell are addicted to illegal drugs, thus drug-free prisoners are affected by the influences of the dealers' power throughout units and are also bullied by their drug-user inmates to whom they are indebted.

Drugs in prison are considered an opportunity to exercise power over one's as well as others' daily life as prisoners. It is also the most profitable business. The network of drugs in prison is a target of power, and it is the only way to control the life of prisoners, who are provided with opportunities to express their desires for using or selling drugs, which, in turn, makes it easier for those in power (i.e. managers of prisons) to recognize, categorize, and identify prisoners and control them. Social behaviors of prisoners revolve around drugs; their functionality rests on drugs. Therefore, instead of managing prisoners by employing educated correctional officers and rehabilitation programs, managers of prisoners relied on drugs as a multitasking tool. Controlling prisoners with minimum rehabilitation facilities in prison could not be possible except with the constant use of drugs. It is the most cost-effective and profitable strategy to use in managing a prison. Although some of the violence in prison is directly affected by drugs, regulating drug networks decreases violence overall. Using illegal drugs is a beneficial strategy to control the protests and violence in prison through controlling the prisoners' bodies and minds. High-status drug dealers do have ultimate power over an inmate's life; thus, constant negotiation and trade between the correctional officers and them makes the control mechanism more efficient and accessible.

> *All guards know who delivers drugs to the prison; this is exactly what they want.* (Male participant, five years of incarceration)

> *All protests can be shut down by distributing drugs in the prison.* (Male participant, nine years of incarceration)

> *Fighting in prison is decreased by distributing drugs. Prisoners have to be kept busy by drugs and gambling.* (Male participant, five years of incarceration)

All of the prisoners in our cell, about 80 people, used heroin. Even the wardens were witnessing our drug consumption in the yard and did not care at all. (Male participant, nine years of incarceration)

Methadone was also considered a control mechanism in prison, and it was distributed among prisoners constantly via the medical center of the prison. Almost all inmates considered methadone another addictive drug.

If we did not use methadone in prison, there was a fight every day. Methadone was distributed to calm down prisoners. (Male participant, five years of incarceration)

Methadone was distributed in prison at a specific time of day. Methadone was distributed among prisoners for three reasons: 1. To medicate people who use drugs, 2. To make them calm, and 3. To decrease the risk of shared injections and HIV. Not only do they use methadone but also all other kinds of drugs. (Male participant, nine years of incarceration)

Prisoners' behaviors and actions can be more predictable if they use illegal drugs. They become passive objects in prison as in society before their incarceration. Their dependency on illegal drugs continues in custody as well, and it might even increase as a result of having no communication with family members. The only thing that they can count on in prison is drugs.

It was impossible to cut the drugs from the prison, and no matter what section of the prison you were in you could find syringes. In our section, there were 700 prisoners who were all heroin addicts. If they did not have heroin, they turned into monsters. So, how could guards control them? Just by controlling the transfer of drugs into prison. (Male participant, ten years of incarceration)

Five years ago, a prison's warden decided to abandon drugs in the prison; there were a lot of protests against this decision and a lot of people were killed. Then, they did not ever abandon drugs. They found out that prisoners are more manageable by using drugs than without them. (Male participant, seven years of incarceration)

For drug traffickers, society is like prison and prison is like society. In terms of economic gains, however, selling drugs in prison was far more profitable. The penal world functions as the most economically secure region with the greatest profit for dealers. In other words, through incarcerating people who use drugs, the most profitable business is organized. A former prisoner declared:

The best-quality drugs with the highest price have been transferred to the prison, just to control prisoners. (Male participant, nine years of incarceration).

Officers play a pivotal role in keeping this network alive in the heart of the prison. In prison, the only law ruling the drug network is, the more addicts are imprisoned, the more profit is obtained. Exclusively selling drugs at the highest price and always in one area is more manageable than in the outside world. There are no competitors in prison, so the drug business lies in the hands of the most powerful prisoners who earn the most profit. It is cost effective in terms of transportation as well, as it takes only around five minutes to transfer drugs from one cell to another or from one section to another.

You can buy drugs in the prison quicker and easier than outside; if it takes one hour to buy drugs outside, it takes just one minute to buy and use drugs inside the prison. (Male participant, nine years of incarceration)

If there was no bread in the prison, you could just use hashish instead. (Male participant, seven years of incarceration)

I remember that guards discovered about 10 kilograms of opium just in one section of the prison. (Male participant, four years of incarceration)

Also, officers' cooperation makes the process more convenient.

It felt so bad to admit the fact that all prisons' managers tend to distribute drugs in the prison. They themselves kept some doors open to allow drug transferring to the prison. The most important reason was that, for example, in our section, there were about 400 prisoners without any sign of hope in their faces; their family members were not there to support them emotionally. Most of them did

> *not have any visits from their family. Along with that, the prisoners, cell mates, and guards do not have that much capacity to support each other. Thus, the only thing to keep them calm was drugs.* (Male participant, six years of incarceration)

Although property and strip searching (i.e. physically examining prisoners while naked) of inmates, especially drug users, happen regularly as a deterrent, the prevalence and use of illegal drugs in prison is an inevitable phenomenon. Also, in a case of searching or inspecting the units in prison, non-drug users are pressured to hide cellmates' drugs, since they are not suspected by officers. Different coercion strategies such as offering a pack of cigarettes or a telephone card were used to persuade them. There are three main routes for trafficking drugs into the prison: prisoners, corrupt officers, and visiting family members. Being in and out of prison by leave or furlough, prisoners import drugs into the prison for their personal consumption. Also, a group of prisoners who are recruited by violent criminals import drugs for their boss. Additionally, some inmates apparently expose themselves intentionally to be arrested so they can be inside the prison and sell drugs.

> *Some prisoners just set up a fake scene to be arrested and sell drugs in the prison to afford their family life outside of the prison.* (Male participant, nine years of incarceration)

> *Kurdish prisoners are well known for delivering drugs by storing them in their body. They made fake scenes to get arrested and sell drugs and then get released. They come with just 50 grams of opium and get released with a large box of money.* (Male participant, four years of incarceration)

> *Some prisoners do not want to be released. They want to stay and sell more drugs and earn money. The price of one gram of methamphetamine is $100 CAD, so it is worth it to stay there.* (Male participant, six years of incarceration)

> *The price of drugs was 20 times more expensive than outside. Even the price of one pack of cigarettes was 10 times more expensive than outside. There were several on-leave prisoners who stored drugs in their bodies. The unit leader was one of the most common drug dealers in the prison, but the point was that due*

> *to his position (the manager of a cell) he was not identified by officers. Also, through any linkage between the prison and outside such as a 'health centre', we import drugs through the inmates who are recruited there. Once someone delivered drugs to the prison, first, he had to give a share to a high-status inmate, and then he kept the rest for himself.* (Male participant, eight years of incarceration)

In addition, family visits were used to pass drugs between family members, especially spouses and parents, to prisoners while hugging or kissing them or putting the drugs into a box containing food or clothes. Prisoners can hide the drugs under the carpet in the visit room, and then, the inmate whose duty is to clean up the room would deliver the drugs or hide them in their body before returning to the cells. The main purpose of this drug transfer through family channels was not personal consumption; rather, it was a way to support financially the prisoners and their family members.

The punishment for deliberate homicide according to Islamic Law is the death penalty (*qisas*) or payment of blood money (*diyat*).[8] Thus, for those inmates who were sentenced to death and the victim's relatives do not insist on *qisas*, the best way to earn enough for blood money was by selling drugs in prison. Given the high price of drugs in prison, families pass drugs to inmates to afford the payment.

> *My mother imported drugs to prison to help me financially. I wanted to sell the drugs to earn money and afford my life in prison and to pay some portion of my debts and afford the payment of blood money. I stored them in my body where it couldn't be searched. After that, every time my mother brought me drugs. But that was so risky, because sometimes we are strip searched, and the officers may find that.* (Female participant, seven years of incarceration)

[8] "In cases of deliberate homicide, *diyat* is due only when the nearest relatives of the victim do not insist on *qisas* .... Whenever the relatives insist upon the payment of *diyat*, it is to be in the value of one hundred camels..... Although *diyat* is originally fixed in terms of camels, it is almost universally admitted that it can be paid by an equivalent amount of money, either gold or silver, cows, sheep or garments" (Pervin 2016, p. 145).

Prisoners are not the only group who make a living through selling drugs in prison; sometimes employees are also involved in this business of importing drugs into the prison.

Even the employees and guards delivered drugs into the prison to earn money. They earned a lot of money by transferring drugs. The money they earned was much more than their salaries." "It is one source of money. Guards deliver drugs to prison and make huge amounts of money. By delivering 50 grams of heroin, which cost US$37outside, they earn US$370 inside. (Male participant, eight years of incarceration)

Employees in the prison themselves deliver drugs into the prison. Last time, one of the employees delivered one kilogram of heroin into the prison. (Male participant, six years of incarceration)

It was unbelievable when I heard that one of the highest-status managers in the prison transferred 600 grams of heroin to the prison. He actually provides drugs for one of the prisoners just for money. (Male participant, eight years of incarceration)

Multidimensional Identity

Recriminalization

When the last objective of prisons is rehabilitation and treatment, all efforts of prisoners are dedicated to entertaining themselves to survive the prison's circumstances. The most popular forms of entertainment among prisoners are bragging about their criminal skills and escapades while socializing and taking drugs simultaneously. The lack of a rehabilitation program is compensated by the re/criminalization process.

Prison is the best educational workshop ever. All prisoners talked about their criminal activities and others were all ears to learn. I got put in prison because of a car robbery, and I got released with enough knowledge about housebreaking. (Male participant, three years of incarceration)

Even violent criminals who were supposed to have several contacts with criminals before incarceration admitted that the prison experience is incomparable with the knowledge they gained among street criminals.

> *I was an active criminal for ten years and got imprisoned more than 32 times. The information and experience I can get from one conversation with a violent criminal in prison cannot be obtained by being ten years outside the prison. Although I played soccer with a box of heroin, which my dad put in my hat for delivery, it did not make me a fearless person, but the prison totally turned me into a fearless criminal. (Male participant, four years of incarceration)*

Inmates with longer sentences who accept the prison as their home become more professional in breaking laws than criminals outside of the prison. Inmates maintain their drug habits and deal drugs more quickly, more profitably, and in even greater quantities than before incarceration. In other words, drugs are used and delivered under the close surveillance of educated correctional officers, thus it would be easier to maintain this habit after being released in society. Although some guards and officers cooperate with prisoners inside the prison in terms of transferring drugs, it happens under close security controls. Not only are prisoners being educated in criminal skills, but they also become capable of practicing those skills in the most secured place, (i.e. prison). Thus, it becomes much easier to traffic drugs outside prison without the constant control of officers and guards.

> *Since I was imprisoned, I have become more professional in criminal activities. I break the law in the prison in the heart of the law, so it is much easier for me to commit crimes outside. When I can transfer drugs from one section of the prison to another section fearlessly under the close control of guards from morning to evening with no chance of escape, transferring drugs outside is as simple as drinking water.* (Male participant, ten years of incarceration)

> *After the few months I was in the prison, I got used to the circumstances and was not scared anymore. So, I started all my habits and behaviours before I was incarcerated. All criminal behaviours get repeated there. Everything formed again with the same quality but with the one exception that I was in prison and*

not in society anymore. We found drugs through any possible paths in the prison. (Male participant, eight years of incarceration)

In women's prison and at socializing times, incarcerated women tend to talk about not only their criminal records, but their sexual relationships outside of the prison as well, especially if their partner was a well-known drug trafficker.

Most of the time they were talking about their sexual relationships with this guy and that guy. They tried to show off in front of other prisoners by describing their sexual relationships with popular drug traffickers. (Female participant, two year of incarceration).

Even prisoners who were trained to carry out political assassinations adapted to the prison subculture.

The guy who assassinated Sayad Shirazi[9] *was in our cell. He was incarcerated in solitary confinement for 2 years. He did not have any visitors. He was not supposed to be in our prison and was in our cell because he was considered a political prisoner. But later he became our cellmate for a few months. Once he came to our cell, he did not even smoke cigarettes and he slept at specific times at night. He did not even eat food in the same dishes as anyone else. He had his own restricted and rigid rules. He resisted so hard against all the unwritten rules of the prison, but eventually he gave in. After a while, he became one of the most violent criminals of the prison. He became someone who gambled for more than seven months every night until 2 am.* (Male participant, nine years of incarceration)

Although prisoners who are sentenced to a short-term incarceration due to petty drug offences are not accepted to socialize with others and are not welcome to participate in prison activities (e.g. religion classes, sewing classes), they will become familiar with the criminal culture if they are incarcerated repeatedly.

---

[9] "Ali Sayad Shirazi was assassinated in 1999 while serving as the deputy chief of the Iranian Armed Forces General Staff, the second-highest military office in Iran." https://en.wikipedia.org/wiki/Ali_Sayad_Shirazi.

For someone who spends a lot of time constantly in prison, prisons' rules become more stable in his mind than recidivist ones. Even those who were incarcerated 10 times in their life and were incarcerated for a short period each time become gradually the same as us who were murderers, drug traffickers, or burglars. I mean, finally at the eleventh time, they were incarcerated because of murder, and they were sentenced to death. Then, such men found a status in the prison. (Male participant, seven years of incarceration)

However, there are prisoners who get incarcerated for a short period of time and are not involved in prison society. Most drug addicts who are sentenced due to possessing or delivering drugs are included in this category. They are not even considered human beings; they are forgotten and invisible prisoners who are considered outsiders in prison. However, they are the most vulnerable group who are exposed to the instability and constant changes of prison environment.

I did not learn anything in the prison, neither criminal activities nor carpet weaving. There was not any spot for me. There were prisoners who were there for 10 or even 20 years who always participated in these types of classes with their fellows. They not only never asked me to come, but also if I wanted to, they would not let me in. Nobody counted on us. I did not talk to anybody because they did not even see me. We did not learn anything about the criminal activities because those groups and gangs did not talk to us. In return, when the boss changed, we were the first group who had to obey her new rules. (Female participant, one year of incarceration)

Long-termers are expected to internalize all the requirements of being violent in prison, as one participant described: "Growing a warrior soul in yourself," even if they do not want to be involved in any violent circumstances. In other words, prisoners must practice and adapt to the peripheries of living among violent criminals.

The unwritten rules of jail are that when you arrive in prison, prison becomes your hope home; it is your new reality. So, you must build your life there. You must match and adapt to its culture. I was not the man I've ever been and have never been involved in fights. But there, there were 400 prisoners who were violent. I had to be violent like them. I had to knife people. It was not needed, but the atmosphere expects it. (Male participant, nine years of incarceration)

I was not a violent person, but I was involved in 15 fights during the first two months I was incarcerated. What I mean is that the most important rule in the prison is that you must adapt to the prison conditions. You should grow a warrior soul and consider either guards or other prisoners as enemies. (Male participant, eight years of incarceration)

Prison subculture affects prisoners' language style as well. Although some were already familiar with criminal language, most of them only learned to use this language while incarcerated. Using specific slang among prisoners is a sign of being violent or at least appearing violent.

The style of my speaking changed completely. I started to use different language and sets of words day by day. This showed that I was violent and tough and a long-termer. (Male participant, nine years of incarceration)

People who use drugs are not only exposed to the criminal lifestyle and subculture in prison (recriminalization) but also to different types of drugs (re-drugization). People who use drugs are exposed to a toxic atmosphere in the prison; they become familiar with new types of drugs and are persuaded to follow the drug business in prison. In other words, if a prisoner's drug of choice was unavailable or expensive, another drug or multiple substances were abused. Some people who use drugs become poly-drug addicts, depending on the accessibility and availability of drugs.

I used opium and heroin, but I became familiar with methamphetamine in the prison. (Male participant, seven years of incarceration)

I was addicted to opium, but I became familiar with heroin in prison. (Female participant, one year of incarceration)

I was addicted to crack, but once I got released, I started injecting heroin. (Male participant, two years of incarceration)

I just used hashish before I got imprisoned, but while in there I used all available drugs. (Female participant, three years of incarceration)

Although Moradi et al. (2015) emphasize the constructive effects of prison-based methadone maintenance treatment to decrease drug abuse in prison and reduce shared injections, the prevalence of using other drugs, even injection of drugs other than methadone, was the clearest message of most participants in the current study. Even non-addicts or recovering addict inmates registered to receive methadone to decrease their anxiety and stress.

> *I tried methadone in prison for the first time, because methamphetamine was 10 times more expensive than outside. Once I was released, I started to use methadone and methamphetamine simultaneously.* (Female participant, three years of incarceration)

Rehabilitation

According to Vaughn and Sapp (1989, p. 73), "custody is taking precedence over rehabilitation, leaving treatment providers with little moral or financial support. Due to budget restraints and burdensome overcrowding issues, treatment modalities are not receiving high priority from lawmakers." One of the consequences of the war on drugs in Iran[10] is considering prison as a punitive institution to create a healthier society rather than treating it like a rehabilitative program. Thus, the custody/treatment duality pushes us to accept Martinson's (1974) hypothesis that "nothing works." Although prisoners are provided with limited rehabilitation programs that specifically concentrate on drug treatment and rehabilitation for violent criminals, those opportunities act as turning points in the lives of few prisoners. *Narcotics Anonymous* (NA) plays a significant role in the spiritual transformation of some prisoners. The coexistence of criminal subculture and NA subculture in the prison creates multiple identities inside recovering inmates in the penal system. NA runs a program weekly in the prison in addition to their rehab centers in the society; almost all NA recovering addicts who have an incarceration history

---

[10] The information related to the "war on drug" in the Islamic Republic of Iran has been extracted from my doctoral dissertation titled "Prison Subculture and Drug-Related Crimes in Iran," in 2019, at Memorial University, Canada.

became volunteers to present and introduce the program in the prison. Although correctional officers did not believe that NA principles could be understood by prisoners, some violent criminals changed their lives forever by participating in NA sessions.

> *Guards did not believe in the function of NA in prison. They told us that prisoners do not understand the NA principles.* (Male participant, nine years of incarceration)

It is not only correctional officers who did not believe in the function of NA in the penal system. Almost all prisoners did not believe in the effectiveness of NA, either, and declined to attend the sessions.

> *In our section, there were 400 prisoners, and fewer than 10 prisoners attended the program. In fact, from those 10 prisoners, just three of them came to the program every week, and the rest of them came rarely. Prisoners are not well-informed about the principles of the program unless they attend the class. In fact, making different rumors and jokes around NA holds some prisoners back from attending this program. We made a joke about the NA meetings and the members in the prison. Instead of Narcotics Anonymous, we called them Soldier Anonymous. I did not attend any NA meetings in the prison as I was afraid of being sent to the forced labor camp. Some prisoners heard of NA's influence in quitting drugs, and thus they decided to attend the sections.* (Male participant, seven years of incarceration)

Spreading the subculture of NA through recovering prisoners creates a contradictory atmosphere; prisoners thus practiced NA principles and struggled with the criminal subculture in prison at the same time.

> *It was a well-known idiom in the prison that 'even the gazelle does not feed his child' (nobody cares about anybody) in the prison; however, we as NA members in the prison attempted to encourage prisoners not to return to the prison again. We actually tried to expand their horizons in the prison. I was a manager in one cell in the prison; I told all the prisoners in the cell that nobody has a right to smoke even one cigarette in this cell. I told them on any occasion that you are not allowed to fight, just have a dialogue. They were not allowed to sell drugs in the cell. All of them must respect other cellmates' rights. I practiced all NA prin-*

> *ciples in the prison. Also, the number of people who use drugs who overcame addiction in prison is no more than 1 or 2 out of 400 inmates.* (Male participant, seven years of incarceration)

Although, as Crewe (2005) states, drug abuse can be considered "a largely individualistic response" to alleviate the pains of prison life, drug addiction in the prison is part of a social network that creates social capital around inmates or, more specifically, as Mjåland (2014, 2016, p. 159) states, drug abuse has "inclusionary and exclusionary functions." Prisoners form and construct social relationships based on their drug habits, and drug withdrawal decisions within prison are not easily accepted by others, since the social position, which has been structured based on drug abuse, collapses and connections and relationships are jeopardized. As Crewe (2005) states, inmates who quit drugs during their sentences have different social experiences of imprisonment.

> *I became a part of an association in the prison where I could share my thoughts and feelings with them. It was called NA. I had several friends and cellmates in the prison, and we did not have any problems with each other after I participated in NA meetings. I was sick of my friends, and I could not stand them anymore. Once I quit drugs, I remember, I did not know what I was supposed to do with my friends. Every time I came back from the NA sessions, they surrounded me and offered me drugs. They told me to come to use drugs. Fortunately, I was trained by NA to say NO simply and immediately refuse this request. All the prisoners are sick of using drugs, and they have lost everything already in their life, but they could not quit that. My friends did not fight with me during the rehabilitation process in the prison, because I know that they wanted to stop using drugs, but they could not.* (Male participant, nine years of incarceration)

Recovering addicts in prison most often go through the withdrawal process through the NA program, and they have reported restoring relationships with their family members who excluded them during times of addiction. Also, their family members start to communicate and even transfer money into ex-addicts' accounts to show their respect for their withdrawal decisions. In fact, many of the connections lost in the prison due to drug withdrawal can be compensated for by restoring, recovering, and repairing personal relationships with family and friends outside the prison. According to Wacquant (2002, p. 388), prison is only suggested as a "distortive and wholly negative" force, while one can consider it "as a stabilizing and restorative force for relations already deeply frayed by the pressures of life and labor at the bottom of the social edifice."

In addition to the NA program, life skills classes were offered in prisons. These types of classes are often held for long-termers. The main objective of classes was training long-termers to be aware of social and cultural changes in society. Prisoners who are released after ten years of incarceration must be resocialized about the culture of society, which might now be unknown to them. When incarcerated, they replaced the society's culture with the prison subculture step by step. Educating them gradually in prison before being released assists them to analyze the forgotten sets of norms in society.

> *When I got incarcerated, I was just 20 years old. The society was not the same, and also I was so young to be incarcerated and locked in a closed building for 10 years. I did not know anything about relationships between men and women, and once I wanted to figure it out, I murdered someone when I was high, and I got imprisoned. The society got turned upside down for 10 years. The only thing that kept me updated somehow, especially regarding boy/girl relationships, was the life skills class that was held in the prison. Prisoners such as I who were incarcerated at such sensitive ages who did not get a chance to figure out and practice social skills were trained in those educational classes in the prison. They constantly repeated the fact that opposite sex relationships have changed dramatically, and if you see unmarried boys and girls in the street who are hanging out freely, do not lose your control, and do not overreact, because this phenomenon is getting more normal than in the past, I mean 13 years ago.* (Male participant, ten years of incarceration)

It is important to note that prisoners who practice religious rituals being constantly humiliated, excluded, isolated, and labeled by other inmates as a "*Mokhber*" (informant) or those who are not "true believers" but practice in return for receiving advantages from prison officers. However, above all, for some of inmates being sentenced to the death penalty acted as a turning point in their life, changing them into theists, believers, and faithful observants of religion. Or, as Beckford et al. (2016, p. 132) state "being imprisoned has actually helped them to begin praying or to take up prayers again after a long period of interruption." Prisoners are nonbelievers or "sinners" at the time of incarceration; however, they convert to true believers during their imprisonment (Maruna et al. 2006; Clear and Sumter 2002; Thomas and Zaitzow 2006).[11]

> *The fact that the prisoner was a murderer outside in society does not mean that he is inherently destructive and a troublemaker. Such prisoners did not believe in God, and once they were incarcerated, each realized that he is a loser. Prison becomes the end of the road for them, so they are not able to do anything in the prison other than change themselves. In the murderer section, about 300 prisoners were kept there. You cannot imagine that just one prisoner each year got released and three prisoners each week were executed. The first day of incarceration for us is like the first night of the grave. We realized that the game is over right now. We wanted to get back to society and ask forgiveness from the victims. In this section, they know and pray to God more than anyone because they touch God everyday by having witnessed their friend's execution. I prayed every day and asked God to have one day's leave to see my mother for the last time. I knew that I was never going to be released, and that I will be executed sooner or later.* (Male participant, nine years of incarceration)

Instrumental Relationships

Friendship Illusion

According to Liebling and Arnold (2012, p. 416), "interactions between prisoners had little substance: they might 'look OK on the surface', but they were extremely guarded. Prisoners were reluctant to give them the label 'relationships'; there was too much fear involved." Inside the prison where inmates' lives are in the "hands of power," everybody attempts to provide for their own life and survive incarceration. Prisoners plan their acts according to safety and drugs, thus making friends is based on

[11] Religious conversion, specifically conversion to Islam, is a well-known phenomenon in American and European prisons. About 80% of those prisoners who seek faith in the US prisons convert to Islam (Ammar et al. 2004; Waller 2003).

providing safety and obtaining drugs; otherwise, nobody cares about anyone else's life outside this golden rule.

> *I entered the prison while I was yelling and crying. I feared everything that I had heard about prison. I heard that nobody cares about anybody in the prison and 'even the gazelle does not feed her child in prison.' Everything I heard was true. If anyone has a financial problem or if anyone cannot afford anything, even food, and has indigestion, nobody cares. Everybody minds their own business.* (Male participant, four years of incarceration)

All rules and relationships in prison are based on needs, verbalized in concepts such as trust, friendship, and respect. Prisoners deal with instrumental relationships in prison, which are based on interim arrangements, matching pairs, and meeting basic needs. It is important to remember that the rare trust, solidarity, respect, and relationships established in the prison all are for the sake of drugs and safety; in other words, they are based on mutual advantages. Inmates repeatedly testified that they were aware of the nature of respect and power in the prison. They declared that personal possessions and power bring respect until high-status inmates meet prisoners' needs.

> *You cannot have that much solidarity in the society outside, as this solidarity is unbreakable for the sake of drugs. The reason behind the constant presence and prevalence of drugs in the prison is just the solidarity of prisoners who prevent any disclosure, and any solidarity is based on protecting and providing drugs.* (Male participant, eight years of incarceration)

Relationships in temporary societies are not based on any other purposes than the fulfillment of basic needs, because everyone is attempting to survive. Thus, relationships in the prison are usually temporary arrangements, especially among short-termers. Their relationships are limited to incarceration periods and last no longer.

> *"I made friends in the prison, but those relationships vanished once I got released." "All my friendships in prison were like a fog; once I was released, they all disappeared."* (Male participant, four years of incarceration)

Being involved in "fragile" relationships in prison depends on the duration of incarceration. Inmates often prefer to communicate and socialize with prisoners with long acquaintanceships through either a long length of imprisonment or previous incarceration experiences. Additionally, inmates consider the social background (e.g. financial status, the prisoner's home region) and the criminal history of other inmates before choosing them. Usually, new prisoners, especially those who are serving less than six months, are not appropriate to be mates. There is just one exception: if the new prisoner is rich or has drugs, he or she gets some attention. Even in this case, a new prisoner is not allowed to distribute or use drugs without the permission of the main distributor of drugs in the prison.

In some rare cases, prisoners manage to keep relationships with each other even after being released; sometimes they become members of the same gang who decide to be criminal partners.

> *When I was released, I found my cellmates for a bank robbery.* (Male participant, five years of incarceration)

Most often, long-termers who were sentenced to life imprisonment and the death penalty kept relationships with their friends even after getting a chance to be released. Prison is a home for long-termers, and even if they get released, they maintain relationships with other prisoners. In addition, there are prisoners who became members of NA in prison and continued their relationships with other NA members in the prison and outside once they were released.

> *I was incarcerated for 10 years. I had a good relationship with the NA members in the prison, as there were only four of us. We are still in contact with each other even after being released. All NA members in the prison keep their relationships with other members after incarceration."* (Male participant, ten years of incarceration)

Also, prisoners make friends with prisoners with the same criminal history as themselves. It is risky to make friends with short-termers since they will leave the prison sooner or later, before becoming known.

Therefore, making friends with prisoners in the same categories increases the chance of meeting a prisoner's basic needs, from safety to drugs.

> *Prisoners who committed violent crimes never ever made friends with us. They did not care about us. They always made friends with the same criminal categories as themselves.* (Male participant, four years of incarceration)

> *It was not safe to have any contacts with the short-termers, since they still did not know prison rules and posed the strong possibility that they would break the rules and create problems for you.* (Male participant, seven years of incarceration)

Long-termers keep their relationships in a gray zone (i.e. "the status that is neither white nor black; living with others in a 'no peace no war' situation") to make the incarceration period tolerable. The most important reason behind keeping relationships in the gray zone is mutual needs. They must deal with each other for the sake of safety and drugs as long as they are living in the prison. Additionally, relationships and making friends with the cellmates act as a backup plan in case of fighting. It is not just obtaining drugs that keeps relationships in a gray zone, as safety is another reason.

> *It is better to have some relationships with your cellmates in the prison just in case. If you have enemies in the prison and you do not have any friends, you are a dead body. You must have friends to stand up for you. Most prisoners just make friends based on being scared about fighting alone.* (Male participant, seven years of incarceration)

Double-Edged Sword

Most prisoners belong to a gang in prison. These gangs are based on different regions in the city and different criminal histories; however, their home region before incarceration play a crucial role in the requirements of a gang. Gangs in prison vary from 30 to 50 individuals. Almost all the gangs in the prison are named after a region in the city; for example, there is a region north of Isfahan called *Sabzemeydon*, and there is a gang in

Isfahan prison with this specific name. These gangs can be categorized into two categories: the upper-class districts and the lower-class districts. It is not necessarily the rule that the upper-class regions take control of the prison or have the power to compete with lower-class district gangs. This all depends on the number of violent criminals in each gang. As one participant stated about the Isfahan prison,

> *For years, the lower-class district gangs had control of the prison and set their own rules to manage the prison; however, recently, the upper-class district gangs had taken control. The upper-class district gangs in Isfahan introduced a new version of illegal drugs and new criminal skills, and through their knowledge, they controlled the whole prison.* (Male participant, ten years of incarceration)

Prisoners are advised to join their own regional gangs to receive all the privileges of the group. If the prisoners prefer to join the other regions' gangs just because they have power or control over others, they will not have the gang's support in a fight. In other words, joining another region's gang is perceived as a betrayal. As a matter of fact, those prisoners are under the close control of not only their own region's gangs, but also the gangs they joined without specific affiliation; in case of fighting or conflicts, the first who will be alone and will be the target of violence are these unaffiliated prisoners. Struggling with gang violence and drug trafficking are inseparable parts of being a member of a gang. Although the concept of the gang is connected with violence behind bars, being a gang member automatically brings emotional and economic support, safety, and further aggression and coercion. Violence and safety are two sides of the same coin. Gangs consisting of members with the most violent criminals and high status can take control over the prison. In fact, having many violent criminals in a gang gives credit to all members of that gang.

> *There was a gang in prison that was originally from* Sabzemeydon *in Isfahan, and they took control of the prison for years, solely because its members were the most violent criminals in the prison. No prisoners dared to disobey those gang members who had been in the prison for years.* (Male participant, ten years of incarceration)

Gaps between safety and violence get blurred daily in prison, so much so that it makes it difficult to recognize them separately. None of these concepts are fully recognizable in the penal world, as their boundaries disappear. Violence for the sake of safety and safety for the sake of violence create multiple identities among prisoners. Each member of a gang is supported emotionally based on their status in the hierarchy of the gang. Most often, the high-status gang members expect to receive more psychological and emotional support from the rest.

> *Like ordinary life outside the prison that requires emotion, money, and affection, the boss of the section demands all of them in the prison from the prisoners. Prisoners who are under his control have to provide all of these qualities for them.* (Male participant, five years of incarceration)

Being a gang member is like living in a safe ship in a stormy sea. The ship provides a safe environment for the members, even if this safety is fragile. Thus, it provides its members with psychological and emotional support.

> *It is an important fact that you have to join gangs of your own region (district). For example, if you are from southeast of Isfahan, the rational decision is that you will join their gang and be a part of their group instead of joining other groups. If any fighting and conflicts happen against you in the prison and you are in a gang that does not inherently belong to you, you will be injured and hurt bad. In fact, in this particular situation, there is nobody to support you, and all of the prisoners who come from the same region will keep each other's back, and you will be left alone with no supporters.* (Male participant, seven years of incarceration)

Being a member of a gang brings identification, a sense of belonging, and status in prison.

> *I was in my uncle's gang in the prison, because I needed their emotional support. I felt safe among them. They gave me an identity, and I was not empty in the prison anymore. They approved of me, whatever I did.* (Male participant, seven years of incarceration)

Some of the prisoners did not have any contact with their family members and friends in society, as most of them were forgotten by their family. Thus, being a gang member created a sense of family for them and gave them support.

> *I did not have anyone. Nobody called me while I was in the prison. They all hated me. I was an addict and hurt them so much. I deserved this misery. But the only chance I had was the gang, and I found myself there. My true identity, I found myself there. They approved of me. All of them were the same as me. I did not feel excluded anymore.* (Male participant, four years of incarceration)

Gangs in prison use their power to apply coercion and aggression to other gangs in the prison, especially those gangs who store drugs in their cells. Analyzing interviews indicated the fact that the emergence of gangs in Iranian prisons does not occur only because of applying coercion and aggression over others, gaining economic support, and being protected from violence; rather, it reveals that men also have emotional and physiological needs. By being a gang member, safety comes in a package that contains family, identity, emotional support, and a sense of belonging that surrounds prisoners in a dangerous world. Therefore, gangs in prison function as a double-edged sword. On the one hand, the members receive belonging, a sense of identity, and emotional support, while at the same time they are threatened by coercion and aggression from other gangs.

Although there are no gangs in women prisons, family-like relationships have various similarities in terms of their function in comparison with gangs in men's prisons. Different familial groups with different statuses coexist in prison; however, one or two families have others under their control. Familial groups resemble the family system in society and consist of grandmothers, mothers, and sisters in the prison. The size of familial groups in women's prison varies; however, they usually had no fewer than 15 members. Essentially, familial groups in prison act as an emotional and financial shelter[12] for women. The grandmother is always

[12] The familial groups in the women's ward are comparable with the *Komun* in the prisons before the Islamic Revolution. However, the financial aspects of the *Komun* were its salient function rather than the emotional aspects; members of the *Komun* shared gifts and money from their families with others to help everyone survive the severe depravation.

an older prisoner with a high-status position in prison, who is called *nane* (grandma). The most common relationships in the familial groups are mother and daughter relationships, which do not necessarily follow demographic rules. In other words, a mother in the familial group is not necessarily older than a daughter.

> "*We protect each other from being bullied or assaulted by other groups in the prison. Also, we are emotionally attached to each other. We cook on the weekend with each other. Sometimes we borrow some things from our family members in the familial group.*" "*I was a mother of some young girls in the prison, and I always encouraged them to read the Quran and be positive. I tried to protect them. We had emotional ties.*" (Female participant, seven years of incarceration)

Women practice femininity constantly in prison, from expressing maternal feelings to building emotional bonds among themselves to creating a second family. Some of the prisoners had children outside the prison and by acting as a mother in the prison they could fill a void and perform their motherly roles vicariously.

> *I play a role as a mother for 10- and 11-year-old-girls in the prison, and I help them in everything. They are scared, and I am the only one who protects them. They remind me of my own daughters whom I lost years ago due to my actions. I feel really good to have them here.* (Female participant, five years of incarceration)

Mothers not only protected the safety of other members of groups but also commanded and guided them. Prisoners with their children in the prison creates family-like relationships, and these were the most peaceful familial groups in the prison. Although they were controlled and authorized by high-status prisoners, the violence impacting them was lesser than other groups in the prison. Child companionship restrained mothers from any violent behavior; in fact, taking care of children in mother sections became a turning point in their lives and helped them avoid dangerous situations which could jeopardize the children's safety inside the prison. Some of the participants declared that being a member of familial groups in prison not only protects themselves from aggression but also is the best way to exploit and coerce others. Familial groups are the best way for violent criminals to meet their goals in the prison.

> *I was a member of a family in the prison, and our mom ordered us to force someone to buy something for us. We were hungry, so we forced a prisoner who was alone and not a member of any groups to buy food for us." "We did not dare to bully a prisoner who was a member of a familial group in the prison, because they were not alone. They will come back with others." "I was in a family group to have some protection and safety in the prison.* (Female participant, three years of incarceration)

Reconceptualization of Trust

The culture of distrust in the prison force prisoners to have restricted and defined relationships with each other, even with their cellmates or gang members. Although trust is one of the psychological needs of individuals to maintain their mental health and plays a crucial role in mutual relationships and identity formation, all prisoners contended that there is no trust in prison. Trust in prison has its own limits and obligations and in order to stay safe, prisoners avoid trusting anyone. They may trust someone whom they had known before incarceration and with whom they had shared a long relationship.

> *I only trust my friend whom I had known for years on the outside. Also, you can somehow trust someone who you have known for years here in the prison.* (Male participant, four years of incarceration)

> *I had friends in the prison, but our relationships were restricted to buying food and drugs. I do not trust them much more.* (Male participant, seven years of incarceration)

The lack of trust in mutual relationships pushes prisoners toward multiple, sometimes conflicting, identities. Prisoners become more careful about their presentation and personality they show in front of others, which creates struggles and challenges. Living in an environment without trust or with only limited trust puts prisoners in the position of being "the others" at all times. Although they have several relationships to guarantee their safety and drugs, prisoners demonstrate fake identities in front of each other.

> *Friendships in the prison are just in films and don't exist in reality. The foundations of friendships in the prison are not based on trust. You cannot see the tangent tree in the middle of a swamp. It is impossible to trust anyone in the prison. You are not you in prison. You change your personality every second to attract their attention to meet your needs; no more.* (Male participant, ten years of incarceration)

> *You have to make a friend with the walls in the prison, and you have to mind your own business. There is no trust in the prison. We just play different roles to take our drugs or to protect us from aggression.* (Male participant, seven years of incarceration)

This mistrust culture in prison even creeps into the relationships between counselors and prisoners. Although counselors are there to help prisoners with their psychological issues, prisoners do not consider them as trustworthy. There is a center for counseling located inside one of the prison, in 2012, there were four professional counselors. All of them were social workers who focused on the problems and challenges of prisoners with their children outside the prison. Those prisoners who were concerned about their children's circumstances outside the prison talked with social workers, who then talked to managers to take the necessary measures. The point is that there was a two-way untruthful road between the prisoners and counselors; according to interviewees, even in a rare situation in which a prisoner decides to consult with social workers and ask for their help, the social workers do not trust them.

> *The employees and guards in the prison cannot trust any prisoners, and I as a prisoner cannot trust them because they gradually become the same as prisoners. They are no human beings different from the prisoners; all are the same. The only employees I could trust were counselors in the prison. Even those consul-*

> *tants were not someone whom other prisoners trusted because they believed that they wanted to find out what is going on in our lives, and they want to spy on us. So, most of the prisoners did not trust them as well. Also, they believed that consultants do not understand our situation because they have not experienced our life. I was someone with whom prisoners consulted sometimes because I had studied sociology.* (Female participant, five years of incarceration)

Almost all drug addict participants in compulsory camps considered trust to be a rare phenomenon, ridiculous to talk about in such circumstances. The process of arresting people who use drugs suddenly while they are walking in the street and forcing them into the detoxification process, which is an unbearable experience for even those people who use drugs and are willing to quit drugs, does not leave any space for building friendships, let alone trusting relationships. As mentioned earlier, such treatment camps are temporary, and the recovering addicts will be released as soon as they get clean. Although there are some representatives of NA, even in compulsory camps, who assist people who use drugs based on the 12-step program, most of them relapse at the time of leaving the camp. As one of the participants stated, people who use drugs consider the camps not as an alternative to prison but as an alternative type of hell. The relationships in camps are based on meeting daily needs from food to safety. Since finding drugs or even abusing drugs in camps is challenging, there is no hierarchy based on the possession of drugs in camps. Most of the addicts in camps are just people who use drugs and are homeless with no history of criminal violence. No relationships based on providing drugs, money, or trust can be formed in compulsory camps. However, some of the participants state that when people who use drugs are arrested in a specific region, almost all of them know one another, since most are homeless and share similar areas where they abuse drugs and sleep at night. Even in these circumstances, where most of them are familiar with each other, they do not trust or even form deep relationships.

Two Sides of the Same Coin

High-status prisoners who are considered leaders or managers in the inmate social world can take advantage of their social position, either to gain aid or to undermine the prison's social order (Sykes 1958). As suggested earlier, high-status inmates (drug traffickers) are mostly in charge of disorder or disobedience in prison. Prisoners act as correctional officers to control, monitor, and manage the prison. Correctional officers put the responsibility for the prison in the hands of high-status prisoners. They act as police or correctional officers to mitigate violence, which might disrupt the routine of the social system of prison. Although trust is an unstable phenomenon between them, correctional officers trust prisoners to be managed by other prisoners who exert influence and power throughout the prison. Given that most of the prisoners are drug users, drug dealers and traffickers have the greatest influence over them; they are the best targets for correctional officers to manage the prison without their constant intervention. High-status inmates become an active part of the control and surveillance of other inmates.

> *I did not see guards in the prison as, actually, the prisoners manage the prison themselves.* (Male participant, ten years of incarceration)

> *I saw guards just once a week, and the inmates with longer sentences managed the prison. I did not see any managers of the prison. Even in a case of fighting, correctional officers do not tend to interfere.* (Male participant, three years of incarceration)

> *Prisoners fight and are injured so badly, but they solve their problems by themselves and even stitch their wounds and pretend that they were self-inflicted.* (Male participant, two years of incarceration)

The reciprocal relationships between drug traffickers and correctional officers facilitate the flow of drugs into the prison. The absolute cooperation between the prisoners and guards creates a win-win game in which each party makes its own profit.

> *I do not know how prisoners delivered drugs to the prison, as guards even search in the vaginas of women. This might directly relate to officers in the prison.* (Male participant, one year of incarceration)

> *Our cell manager who was a violent criminal. Inmates with longer sentences delivered drugs to the prison and told us that the guards did not notice. That was bullshit.* (Male participant, two years of incarceration)

> *We forced guards to deliver to the prison whatever we wanted. We told them that we were here for years, and you must understand us. In the end, we made them emotional. We found a way to deliver drugs to the prison; for example, we would drop something in the bathrooms to cause clogs and then when the plumber came to the prison, we made friends with him. That was one way to persuade someone from the outside to bring drugs for us because they did not usually physically inspect them. I remember we persuaded a guard to bring vodka for us in the prison, because again they were not physically searched.* (Male participant, seven years of incarceration)

Since wealthy prisoners took part financially in forming the prison structure through meeting the accommodation needs of the prisoners, they all are treated respectfully by officers and are considered as trustworthy negotiation partners for officers.

> *You received respect from judges and guards if you were incarcerated for fraud of one milliard toman, since most probably you are wealthy enough to buy some furniture for prison. (Male participant, three years of incarceration)*

The relationships between guards and prisoners are not restricted to financial matters, as prisoners with exceptional situations received true assistance from the wardens and correctional officers. In general, prisoners on death row are treated kindly by correctional officers. On the day of execution, correctional officers try, in a last-minute attempt, to cancel the capital punishment by asking forgiveness from the plaintiff. When possible, they even provide an opportunity for prisoners to go on leave to try to convince the plaintiff.[13]

> *The prosecutor released me based on his own promise to give me the opportunity to ask for the forgiveness of the plaintiff.* (Male participant, nine years of incarceration)

> *Most of the guards in the prison are concerned about the situation of the prisoners. On execution days, they try to delay the punishment to talk with the complainants for forgiveness.* (Male participant, seven years of incarceration)

> *One of the rituals which is popular among guards before execution is searching to find the family of the victim and begging them not to allow the prisoner to be executed.* (Male participant, nine years of incarceration)

> *Some guards cry with all their hearts when innocent prisoners are executed, and sometimes guards devote a lot of time to delaying the execution of one prisoner with the hopes of getting the satisfaction of the plaintiff.* (Male participant, seven years of incarceration)

On the one hand, correctional officers cooperate with prisoners in a win-win game and also support their release, even if they are on death row; on the other hand, snitches are recruited to decrease prisoners' solidarity and jeopardize the inmates' relationships in prison. Through snitches, the culture of distrust intensifies, which subsequently decreases the sense of solidarity. Whenever correctional officers learn about any possible solidarity or solid friendships between prisoners, they recruit snitches not only to pass information but also to scare prisoners away from each other. Through this strategy, a panopticon (Foucault 1979) is created in inmates' minds, thereby they feel they are constantly being monitored, even in their own beds, by snitches. Prison is controlled and organized through high-status prisoners and also through snitches, who

[13] A similar theme is shown in the film *Beautiful City*, directed by multi-award-winning filmmaker Asghar Farhadi in 2004. Akbar is the main character of this film. He committed murder at the age of 16 and was sentenced to the death penalty. When he reaches age 18, the sentence legally can be carried out, thus he is transferred to the prison and awaits his execution. Meanwhile, a correctional officer in the rehabilitation center along with Akbar's friend try to gain the consent of Akbar's plaintiff to stop the execution, providing an opportunity for Akbar to pay *qisas* instead of being executed. https://m.imdb.com/title/tt0424434/.

are invisible agents of correctional officers. These agents of correctional officers pass the information to the guards, and their needs are met in return. The function of snitches in prison is manipulating prisoners' relationships to prevent them from building trust and to undermine their solidarity.

> *Snitches were set up by guards to decrease the solidarity between prisoners. If a prisoner gets powerful day by day in the prison, snitches received commands from wardens to spread rumors to ruin their reputation to decrease their power.* (Male participant, ten years of incarceration)

One of the explanations for the existence of snitches (*khabarchin*) in Iranian prisons is that they are a consequence of power struggles among inmates. Leaders among prisoners always compete to take the leadership status, change the prison's informal rules, and get the most advantages (e.g. by taking control of drug networks inside the prison). Thus, informants are assigned through administrators, managers, and correctional officers. To maintain surveillance over prisoners and create a panopticon; in other words, to spread instability, mistrust, and uncertainty among inmates. Additionally, they are used to stop powerful leaders from gaining too much authority in prison, which might increase solidarity among inmates and result in a collective action. It is safer to say that one of the functions of informants is to start rumors which would result in moving a prisoner downward in the prison hierarchy. In fact, informants were assigned to disrupt the growing trust and solidarity among prisoners either by disclosing information for managers or by spreading rumors against someone's reputation.

> *In the past, it was up to prisoners to choose their cellmates, but now the new prisoners are allocated to cells by guards, because guards want to put a snitch in each cell. So, whenever a new prisoner came to our cell, the manager of the cell announced the wake-up time sooner so that the regulars encouraged him to leave the room and let us act freely. If he did not go to the yard, we did something to force him to leave.* (Male participant, seven years of incarceration)

In the prison, there were some prisoners who became powerful during the time of incarceration. They committed violent crimes outside in the society and inside of the prison. Also, they transferred drugs from the prison to the outside and from the outside to the prison with the cooperation of guards and managers of the prison. There were so powerful that they had personal and family information on all involved managers and guards in case of disobedience. They were like a mafia; they managed drug trafficking from Shiraz to Zahedan. The warden of the prison realized that most of the guards and managers were involved in this situation, so they decided to spread the rumor that guns were being delivered into the prison. The rumors were spread by snitches, and then police enforcement came to search for the guns. First, they started searching their rooms, and the enforcement guards offended them greatly by searching every spot and separating prisoners into different cells. That was like a spark, as big fighting happened between the police and those prisoners. Police enforcement shot all six prisoners right in their own cell. Since then, managers have been cautious regarding prisoners who have the potential to become powerful in the prison. They started to recruit snitches to prevent the same situation from happening. (Male participant, ten years of incarceration)

References

Ammar, N. H., Weaver, R. R., & Saxon, S. (2004). Muslims in prison: A case study from Ohio state prisons. *International Journal of Offender Therapy and Comparative Criminology, 48*(4), 414–428.

Anaraki, N. R., & Boostani, D. (2014). Mother-Child Interaction: A Qualitative Investigation of Imprisoned Mothers. *Quality & Quantity, 48*(5), 2447–2461.

Beckford, J., Joly, D., & Khosrokhavar, F. (2016). *Muslims in Prison: Challenge and Change in Britain and France.* Springer.

Bezhan, F. (2019). *Women Banned from Cycling in Bike-Friendly Iranian City.* Radio Free Europe.

Bullock, T. (2003). Changing Levels of Drug Use Before, During and After Imprisonment. *Home Office Research Study, 267*, 23–48.

Clear, T. R., & Sumter, M. T. (2002). Prisoners, Prison, and Religion: Religion and Adjustment to Prison. *Journal of Offender Rehabilitation, 35*(3–4), 125–156.

Clemmer, D. (1940). *The Prison Community*. New York: Holt, Rinehart & Winston.
Clemmer, D. (1958). *The Prison Community*. 1940. Reprint. New York: Holt, Rinehart and Winston,
Crewe, B. (2005). Prisoner Society in the Era of Hard Drugs. *Punishment & Society, 7*(4), 457–481.
Crewe, B. (2006). Prison Drug Dealing and the Ethnographic Lens. *The Howard Journal of Criminal Justice, 45*(4), 347–368.
Defina, R. H., & Hannon, L. (2010). The Impact of Adult Incarceration on Child Poverty: A County-Level Analysis, 1995–2007. *The Prison Journal, 90*(4), 377–396.
Eddy, J. M., & Reid, J. B. (2002). The Antisocial Behavior of the Adolescent Children of Incarcerated Parents: A Developmental Perspective. Paper Presented at the From Prison to Home Conference, Washington, DC.
Edgar, K., & O'Donnell, I. (1998). *Mandatory Drug Testing in Prisons: An Evaluation*. Home Office.
European Monitoring Centre for Drugs and Drug Addiction. (2012). *Prisons and Drugs in Europe: The Problem and Responses: Selected Issue 2012*. Publications Office of the European Union.
Foster, H., & Hagan, J. (2007). Incarceration and Intergenerational Social Exclusion. *Social Problems, 54*, 399–433.
Foucault, M. (1979). *Discipline and Punish: The Birth of the Prison*. Vintage.
Friestad, C., & Hansen, I. L. S. (2005). Mental Health Problems Among Prison Inmates: The Effect of Welfare Deficiencies, Drug Use and Self-Efficacy. *Journal of Scandinavian Studies in Criminology and Crime Prevention, 6*(2), 183–196.
Fritsch, T., & Burkhead, J. (1981). Behavioral Reactions of Children to Parental Absence Due to Imprisonment. *Family Relations, 3*(1), 83–88.
Garabedian, P. G. (1963). Social Roles and Processes of Socialization in the Prison Community. *Social Problems, 11*, 139.
Giallombardo, R. (1966). Social Roles in a Prison for Women. *Social Problems, 13*(3), 268–288.
Goffman, E. (1961). *Asylums: Essays on the Social Situation of Mental Patients and Other Inmates*. Routledge.
Hensley, C. L. (1995). *Social Reactance Towards Homosexuality: An Analysis of College Student's Attitudes*.
Hensley, C. L. (2000). Attitudes Toward Homosexuality in a Male and Female Prison: An Exploratory Study. *The Prison Journal, 80*(4), 434–441.

Herek, G. M. (1988). Heterosexuals' Attitudes Toward Lesbians and Gay Men: Correlates and Gender Differences. *Journal of Sex Research, 25*(4), 451–477.
Herek, G. M., & Capitanio, J. P. (1999). Sex Differences in How Heterosexuals Think About Lesbians and Gay Men: Evidence from Survey Context Effects. *Journal of Sex Research, 36*(4), 348–360.
Hissel, S., Bijleveld, C., & Kruttschnitt, C. (2011). The Well-Being of Children of Incarcerated Mothers: An Exploratory Study for the Netherlands. *European Journal of Criminology, 8*(5), 346–360.
Hucklesby, A., & Wilkinson, C. (2001). Drug Misuse in Prisons: Some Comments on the Prison Service Drug Strategy. *The Howard Journal of Criminal Justice, 40*(4), 347–363.
Hungerford, G. (1993). The Children of Inmate Mothers: An Exploratory Study of Children, Caretakers and Inmate Mothers in OHIO. PhD Thesis, The Ohio State University.
Johnson, E. I., & Waldfogel, J. (2002). Parental Incarceration: Recent Trends and Implications for Child Welfare. *Social Service Review, 76*(3), 460–479.
Johnson, R. (2009). Ever-Increasing Levels of Parental Incarceration and the Consequences for Children. In *Do Prisons Make Us Safer? The Benefits and Costs of the Prison Boom* (pp. 177–206). New York: Russell Sage Foundation.
Khoshnood, K., Hashemian, F., Moshtagh, N., Eftekahri, M., & Setayesh, S. (2008). T03-O-08 Social Stigma, Homosexuality and Transsexuality in Iran. *Sexologies, 17*, S69.
Kite, M. E., & Whitley, B. E., Jr. (1996). Sex Differences in Attitudes Toward Homosexual Persons, Behaviors, and Civil Rights a Meta-Analysis. *Personality and Social Psychology Bulletin, 22*(4), 336–353.
Koscheski, M., & Hensley, C. (2001). Inmate Homosexual Behavior in a Southern Female Correctional Facility. *American Journal of Criminal Justice, 25*(2), 269.
Kurdek, L. A. (1988). Perceived Social Support in Gays and Lesbians in Cohabitating Relationships. *Journal of Personality and Social Psychology, 54*(3), 504.
Lamar, L., & Kite, M. (1998). Sex Differences in Attitudes Toward Gay Men and Lesbians: A Multidimensional Perspective. *Journal of Sex Research, 35*(2), 189–196.
Liebling, A. (2013). Identity and Emotion in a High Security Prison: Alison Liebling Considers Prison Research as Emotional 'Edgework'. *Criminal Justice Matters, 91*(1), 22–23.

Liebling, A., & Arnold, H. (2012). Social Relationships Between Prisoners in a Maximum Security Prison: Violence, Faith, and the Declining Nature of Trust. *Journal of Criminal Justice, 40*(5), 413–424.

Lockwood, D. (1980). *Prison Sexual Violence*. New York: Elsevier.

Martinson, R. (1974). What Works? – Questions and Answers About Prison Reform. *Public Interest, 35*(Spring), 22–54.

Maruna, S., Wilson, L., & Curran, K. (2006). Why God is Often Found Behind Bars: Prison Conversions and the Crisis of Self-Narrative. *Research in Human Development, 3*(2–3), 161–184.

Mjåland, K. (2014). 'A Culture of Sharing': Drug Exchange in a Norwegian Prison. *Punishment & Society, 16*(3), 336–352.

Mjåland, K. (2016). Exploring prison drug use in the context of prison-based drug rehabilitation. *Drugs: Education, prevention and policy, 23*(2), 154–162.

Moradi, G., Farnia, M., Shokoohi, M., Shahbazi, M., Moazen, B., & Rahmani, K. (2015). Methadone maintenance treatment program in prisons from the perspective of medical and non-medical prison staff: A qualitative study in Iran. *International journal of health policy and management, 4*(9), 583.

Murray, J., Farrington, D. P., Sekol, I., & Olsen, R. F. (2009). Effects of Parental Imprisonment on Child Antisocial Behaviour and Mental Health: A Systematic Review. *Campbell Systematic Reviews, 5*(1), 1–105.

Nacci, P. L., & Kane, T. R. (1984). Sex and Sexual Aggression in Federal Prisons. *Federal Probation, 48*, 46.

Oleinik, A. (2003). *Organized Crime, Prison and Post-Soviet Societies*. Routledge.

Oleinik, A. (2013). The Social Life of Illegal Drug Users in Prison: A Comparative Perspective. *European Journal of Crime, Criminal Law and Criminal Justice, 21*(2), 185–206.

Oleinik, A. (2016). Honor and Human Rights: A Comparative Study of Russia and Ukraine. *Comparative Sociology, 15*(6), 669–698.

Pervin, M. (2016). Law of Murder Under Islamic Criminal Law: An Analysis. *JL Pol'y & Globalization, 53*, 143.

Plugge-Foust, C., & Strickland, G. (2000). Homophobia, Irrationality, and Christian Ideology: Does a Relationship Exist? *Journal of Sex Education and Therapy, 25*(4), 240–244.

Plugge, E., Yudkin, P., & Douglas, N. (2009). Changes in Women's Use of Illicit Drugs Following Imprisonment. *Addiction, 104*(2), 215–222.

Poehlmann, J. (2005). Children's Family Environments and Intellectual Outcomes During Maternal Incarceration. *Journal of Marriage and Family, 67*(5), 1275–1285.

Price, J., & Dalecki, M. G. (1998). The Social Basis of Homophobia: An Empirical Illustration. *Sociological Spectrum, 18*(2), 143–159.

Richmond, K. (1978). Fear of Homosexuality and Modes of Rationalisation in Male Prisons. *The Australian and New Zealand Journal of Sociology, 14*(1), 51–57.

Saum, C. A., Surratt, H. L., Inciardi, J. A., & Bennett, R. E. (1995). Sex in Prison: Exploring the Myths and Realities. *The Prison Journal, 75*(4), 413–430.

Scharff-Smith, P., & Gampell, L. (2011). *Children of Imprisoned Parents. European Network for Children of Imprisoned Parents*. University of Ulster and Bambinisenzasbarre, The Danish Institute for Human Rights, Denmark.

Seltzer, R. (1992). The Social Location of Those Holding Anti-Homosexual Attitudes. *Sex Roles, 26*(9–10), 391–398.

Sigelman, C. K., Howell, J. L., Cornell, D. P., Cutright, J. D., & Dewey, J. C. (1991). Courtesy Stigma: The Social Implications of Associating with a Gay Person. *The Journal of Social Psychology, 131*(1), 45–56.

Stover, H., & Weilandt, C. (2007). Drug Use and Drug Services in Prison. In *Health in Prisons: A WHO Guide to the Essentials of Prison Health* (pp. 85–111). Copenhagen: WHO Regional Office for Europe.

Strang, J., Gossop, M., Heuston, J., Green, J., Whiteley, C., & Maden, A. (2006). Persistence of Drug Use During Imprisonment: Relationship of Drug Type, Recency of Use and Severity of Dependence to Use of Heroin, Cocaine and Amphetamine in Prison. *Addiction, 101*(8), 1125–1132.

Struckman-Johnson, C., Struckman-Johnson, D., Rucker, L., Bumby, K., & Donaldson, S. (1996). Sexual Coercion Reported by Men and Women in Prison. *Journal of Sex Research, 33*(1), 67–76.

Sykes, G. M. (1958). *The Society of Captives: A Study of a Maximum Security Prison*. Princeton University Press.

Tewksbury, R. (1989). Fear of Sexual Assault in Prison Inmates. *The Prison Journal, 69*(1), 62–71.

Thomas, J., & Zaitzow, B. H. (2006). Conning or Conversion? The Role of Religion in Prison Coping. *The Prison Journal, 86*(2), 242–259.

Trammell, R. (2012). *Enforcing the Convict Code: Violence and Prison Culture*. Boulder, CO: Lynne Rienner Publishers.

Van De Ven, P. (1994). Comparisons Among Homophobic Reactions of Undergraduates, High School Students, and Young Offenders. *Journal of Sex Research, 31*(2), 117–124.

Vaughn, M. S., & Sapp, A. D. (1989). Less Than Utopian: Sex Offender Treatment in a Milieu of Power Struggles, Status Positioning, and Inmate

Manipulation in State Correctional Institutions. *The Prison Journal, 69*(2), 73–89.

Waller, M. (2003). *Terrorist recruitment and infiltration in the United States: Prisons and Military as an Operational Base*. Washington, DC: United States Senate Committee on the Judiciary.

Ward, D. A., & Kassebaum, G. G. (1964). Homosexuality: A Mode of Adaptation in a Prison for Women. *Social Problems, 12*(2), 159–177.

Wacquant, L. (2002). The curious eclipse of prison ethnography in the age of mass incarceration. *Ethnography, 3*(4), 371–397.

West, D. J. (1983). Sex Offenses and Offending. *Crime and Justice, 5*, 183–233.

Wooden, W. S., & Parker, J. (1982). *Men Behind Bars. Sexual Exploitation in Prison*. New York: Plenum Press.

4

Incarcerated Women and Children

Women's Pathway to Prison

Although statistics show the high rates of women incarcerated, gender is a forgotten part of punishment studies, as neglecting and ignoring gender within criminological lines of thought has been pervasive (Simpson 1989) (see Table 4.1).[1] Various scholars have explored different pathways to crime for women (Brennan et al. 2012; Salisbury and Van Voorhis 2009; Javdani et al. 2011; DeHart 2008; Owen and Bloom 2000; Harden and Hill 1998; Simpson et al. 2008; Daly 1992; Miller 1986; Moffitt 1993; Holsinger and Holsinger 2005; Makarios 2007; Richie 1996; Franklin 2008; Fontaine et al. 2009). These pathways are distinctive for women due to their more frequent experiences of sexual and emotional victimization (Simpson et al. 2008; Daly 1992; Salisbury and Van Voorhis 2009), marginalization (Richie 2001), and depression (Calhoun 2001;

[1] "The female prison population rate is calculated on the basis of the national population total. All national population figures are inevitably estimates but the estimates used in the World Prison Brief are based on official national figures, United Nations figures or figures from other recognised international authorities. (If the rate were calculated on the basis of the number of females in the national population it would of course be approximately double the figure in the final column.)" (World Prison Brief, Institute for Crime & Justice Policy Research, 2018).

N. R. Anaraki, *Prison in Iran*, Palgrave Studies in Prisons and Penology,
https://doi.org/10.1007/978-3-030-57169-6_4

Table 4.1 Female prison population trend, published in *World Prison Brief*, Institute for Crime & Justice Policy Research

Country	Year	Number of female prisoners	Percentage of total prison population (%)	Female prison population rate (per 100,000 of national population)
Iran	2002	5790	3.5	8.6
	2014	6880	3.1	8.8
Afghanistan	2004	103	2.0	0.4
	2018	814	2.6	2.3
Iraq	2005	215	2.5	0.8
	2014	1103	2.6	3.2
Poland	2000	1729	2.5	4.5
	2020	3285	4.4	8.7

Belknap and Holsinger 2006) compared with men. In this chapter, I explore five vulnerabilities that are particularly salient in emerging crime among incarcerated women in Iran: family facilitating crime, addiction, escape, exclusion, and a lack of social and family support.[2]

Being a member of a family with substance abuse, lifelong domestic violence, dysfunctional inmate relationships, divorce, patriarchal and hegemonic management, poverty-stricken, and crowdedness lead people toward addiction, temporary marriages, leaving school early, running away from abusive homes, ongoing criminal involvement, and eventually imprisonment. The role of family dysfunction in leading individuals toward deviance, especially girls and women, is crucial (Beaver and Wright 2007; Willis and Rushforth 2003; Javdani et al. 2011; Covington 2002; Dalley 2002). Almost all of the participants in my study were familiar with substance abuse from an early age; in other words, drug abuse was a common and prevalent phenomenon among their family members, which not only makes drugs available, but also provides fertile soil for their engagement and involvement in drug abuse and drug dealing.

[2] Parts of the results and interviews in this section were published in a paper titled "Patriarchy as a contextual and gendered pathway to crime: a qualitative study of Iranian women offenders" (2018), Quality and Quantity International Journal of Methodology.

> *My parents not only used to smuggle drugs, but also, as far as I remember, used to smoke drugs and constantly argue with each other about drugs. My 13-year-old brother also used to smoke drugs at home with his friends. In our home, drugs were so common, like sweet snacks.* (Incarcerated woman, three years imprisoned)

> *My aunt, whose house was near to ours, used to smoke and smuggle drugs. We always used to be with her and see her smoking drugs.* (Incarcerated woman, five years imprisoned)

They experienced or witnessed constant aggressiveness and fighting in their families. Physical violence results in traumatic incidents. As one of the participants described:

> *My parents always used to argue with each other until leading to fighting and hurting each other. One day, my father shoved my mother while fighting; her head hit a platform, and she passed away.* (Incarcerated woman, three years imprisoned)

Also, they were victims of sexual assault, harassment, and abuse, particularly from their brothers, fathers, friends, and partners, which played a pivotal role in their escaping from home and getting divorced. One participant was beaten, harmed, and immured by her addicted husband. According to Sharpe (2013), most offending girls are victims of physical and emotional abuse by their stepfathers or brothers or another male relative, which forces them to run away from home. It is well documented that women offenders have a life-long history of victimization and abuse (Shechory et al. 2011; Dalley 2002; Covington 1998; Zhang et al. 2009; McDaniels-Wilson and Belknap 2008; Green et al. 2005; Wong 2011; Belknap and Holsinger 2006).

> *When I was 14, my brother brought me to his three friends' house. They raped me by force, and my brother was just looking. From then on, once in a while, he used to bring me to his friends by force and punishment. He himself also used to see and enjoy.* (Incarcerated woman, one year imprisoned)

My husband used to smoke meth and hallucinate that I had a relationship with another man. Then, he used to beat me so much that I fainted. Even after I got divorced from him, he immured me for 10 days and tortured me to recant my divorce. (Incarcerated woman, four years imprisoned)

The same story was told by another participant, but, in this case, children were victims of the violation as well. Generally, sexual harassment, physical abuse, aggressiveness, dysfunctional relationships, and addiction are interwoven and reinforce one another.

My second Sigheh[3] *husband, imprisoned my children and me for two months and beat me lest I escape and get divorced.* (Incarcerated woman, four years imprisoned)

Hegemonic strategies and patriarchy were the dominant discourses of participants' families; in other words, family plays a significant role in policing women's behaviors. Females suffer more in their family environments because they live intensively in relationships; thus, the chance that girls will rebel against their family is much higher than for boys. In contrast to the argument that the chance of being a criminal can be mitigated in the case of severe surveillance over women, evidence in the current research reveals that participants under the constant gaze of family more frequently escape home, take illegal drugs, or hang out with friends to relieve their stress and pain. Women in this study were not involved in or even consulted about crucial events in their lives such as marriage. In cases in which they decided to ask about suitors or potential options for marriage, they were accused of being a whore or impatient to have a sexual relationship with men. In most cases, the potential suitors were addicted, involved in drug-related crimes, or had a father or brother who was also addicted. A compulsory marriage with addicted criminals was common in women offenders' lives.

I had many suitors, but my family never introduced even one of them to me. When I asked them who he was, my mother used to insult me and say, 'You ask

[3] Short-term marriage in Islam.

> *because you want to have sex or become pregnant?' They themselves used to decide to say no to the suitors.* (Incarcerated woman, five years imprisoned)

> *A boy came as a suitor, and the entire neighborhood knew he was an addict and a felon. I also hated him, but my brothers forced me to marry him. So, I got married with him by force; otherwise, my brothers would have killed me.* (Incarcerated woman, four years imprisoned)

Developing and supporting drug habits through prostitution and drug dealing were pervasive among incarcerated women. Family and friends were not the only resources for being exposed to drugs, as running away from abusive homes and being labeled as street women led them into the street men's traps. Entering into the so-called men's world of the streets pushed women unintentionally toward committing illegal activities and being involved in temporary and premature marriages to afford their life, which resulted in being excluded permanently from their family, who, interestingly, were the primary source of deviance for the escaped women. Akram was a woman who witnessed constant fights over the divorce between her parents and was under severe control by her military dad until she decided to set herself free.

> *At home, there was always a challenge between my parents for separation. In addition, every day, my father used to argue and fight with me about with whom I go and come; I was so tired of that... till he found a cigarette in my pocket and just beat me, so I escaped from home. I was living on the street and sleeping in a car for several months until I started to sell drugs to rent a place for myself to live. I fell in love with a man who was drug addicted as well. I decided to return to my home and be with my family and then get married to that guy. However, the story of the same surveillance, the same obligations, the same fights and not being accepted by my family members forced me to escape again. Again, I returned home by accepting to get married to a guy that I did not like, someone who I killed him eventually with the help of my boyfriend.* (Incarcerated woman, three years imprisoned)

Incarcerated women were labeled, excluded, isolated, and deprived of having a "normal" life and trapped into a cycle of strain that involved sexual and emotional abuse, severe surveillance, aggressiveness, divorce, temporary marriages, a lack of family support, labeling, exclusion, and incarceration.

> *The story of my escape from home is still told among my relatives. When something used to happen, they immediately used to carp about the escape of Amir and me in my family; on the other hand, my family constantly used to insult me… even when I got imprisoned, I asked them if they could take my child or not. They answered, 'the relatives would ask us where the mother of this child is. We don't do it; how can we respond to the relatives?!' My mother and sister used to come to my house and constantly speak sarcastically about my life and insult me. My mother used to say, 'Your sabotages have caused no one to come as a suitor for your sister; you've ruined all our lives.* (Incarcerated woman, five years imprisoned)

Incarcerated Mothers

The number of imprisoned women is increasing drastically (Flynn 2012; Kruttschnitt and Gartner 2003; Hagan and Dinovitzer 1999; Mumola 2000; Poehlmann 2005), and, subsequently, the number of affected children is growing as well (Seymour 1998). In many countries, there is a lack of information about the number of children with incarcerated parents (Murray et al. 2009; Flynn 2012). Although there is no transparent official information about the number of children in prison in Iran, according to Mohammad Javad Fathi, a member of parliament, there were over 2300 children living in prison with their mothers in 2017. There is contradictory information available regarding the number of children who live with their mothers in prison in Iran. According to Children of Imprisoned Parents International, there were 450 children residing in prison with their mothers in 2008, 425 in 2015, and 200 in 2017; it is not clear that this reduction in children in prison is a result of changing policies or the provision of childcare facilities outside prisons. Meanwhile, Sahindokht Molaverdi (2015), a deputy in women's and family affairs, has stated that there are 200 children in prison.

Imprisoned women face numerous challenges compared with men, not just because they are victims of stigmatization and social exclusion, but due to their relationships with their children. More women are responsible for taking care of children than men, which makes it significantly more difficult for them to adjust to incarceration circumstances. A lack of reliable statistical relevant information about children (e.g. numbers, ages, health issues, educational needs) in prison shows how deeply their needs in prison are neglected by authorities. We still know little about mother-child interactions and their impacts on their lives in Iran. Only limited research has been done on this topic, with most of it focusing on the circumstances of children of incarcerated mothers behind the walls.

Studies on children of incarcerated mothers fall into two groups: those focused on the companionship between children and their mothers into prison (Pösö et al. 2010; Eloff and Moen 2010; Celinska and Siegel 2010; Kochal and Shamai 2008; Ferrara et al. 2007; Catan 1992; Hartz-Karp 1983) and those that concentrate on separated children (Fritsch and Burkhead 1981; Poehlmann 2005; Eddy and Reid 2002; Hagan and Dinovitzer 1999; Hissel et al. 2011; Foster and Hagan 2007; Hungerford 1993; Johnson 2009; Johnson and Waldfogel 2002; Murray et al. 2009; Scharff-Smith and Gampell 2011; DeFina and Hannon 2010). Various studies describe the logic of keeping young children with their mothers in prison (Cunninham 2001; Robertson 2007) as well as the side effects of them living in prison (Villanueva et al. 2009). It is well documented that the future mental health of children depends on the quality of parental care in their early ages (Bowlby 1952); the attachment of infants to parents will be damaged if there is a lack of regular and sustained contact between them (Parke and Clarke-Stewart 2002); physical, intellectual, behavioral, and emotional damage will be expected for infants with maternal depravation (Steele 2008); and the development of a healthy sense of the child's identity depends on receiving a proper response from parents when they ask for help (MacBride 2008).

In many countries around the world, children and infants reside in prison with their mothers. Some countries provide them with mother-child residential units and programs to mitigate the side effects of incarceration on children. In Iran children aged three or younger (this age varies in different prisons, from infants to children of six years old) are allowed to live with their mothers in prison. However, no special accommodations seem to be provided, except kindergarten in some prisons, which results in hampering the child's social and emotional development. Mothers and children in prisons are kept in regular cells like other criminals with no special accommodations.

In the following sections, I will depict mother-child interactions inside[4] and outside[5] of prison. I am interested in revealing how the exercising of repressive power poisons the children of incarcerated mothers as well, regardless of their presence in the prison. We know little about mother-child interactions inside prisons, especially in the Islamic Republic of Iran, where prisons are a "closed" field of study.

It is assumed that the primary goal of keeping children with mothers in prison is to protect the children's rights, strengthen their emotional attachments, and enhance their bonding, which are crucial in a child's emotional and cognitive development. However, incarcerated mothers, law enforcement, and prison authorities apparently profit more compared to children. The most significant reason is a lack of child-mother accommodations or alternative prison programs in Iranian prisons, as mothers and children live among other prisoners and share the same facilities. The necessity of mother-child interactions for child development coupled with mothers' rehabilitation reveals that considering alternative programs is significant. Being a mother in prison provides women with a positive identity, a source of emotional support, and peace of mind. The positive impacts of mother-child interactions inside prisons for incarcerated mothers have been well documented (Juliette 2008; Celinska and Siegel 2010; Hartz-Karp 1983; Pösö et al. 2010). Additionally, children's presence in prisons facilitates the pathway to

---

[4] Parts of the results and interviews in this section were published in a paper titled "Mother–child interaction: a qualitative investigation of imprisoned mothers", (2014b), Quality and Quantity International Journal of Methodology.

[5] Parts of the results and interviews in this section were published in a paper titled "Living in and living out: a qualitative study of incarcerated mothers' narratives of their children's living condition", (2014a), Quality and Quantity International Journal of Methodology.

rehabilitation as well (Socorro 2009; Baunach 1985). They are freely provided with the most available medicine to cure their anxiety, sadness, anger, and depression, which they have experienced since they were children in a dysfunctional family. Even mothers who were on death row tolerated the stress of being executed and were more mentally stable through the magic of the maternal bond.

> *As I found out that my punishment could be life imprisonment or execution, I was devastated. But when my baby smiled at me, everything changed. He helped me not to get depressed.* (Incarcerated woman, three years imprisoned)

Being a troublemaker and fighting with other inmates was described as part of the day-to-day life of incarcerated women. However, shifting a focus away from the "pains of imprisonment" could be possible by serving time with a child. Mojgan was a participant who was incarcerated twice; however, she served the second time with the company of her child.

> *If I am separated from my child, I will have to be in quarantine since I am nervous, and I will become angry soon. The only thing that makes me calm is my child. The first time I was in prison without my kid, I was mischievous, spending my time in the yard, making trouble. But with my child, I am at ease. At ease enough for all people to count on me.* (Incarcerated woman, three years imprisoned)

Incarcerated women who were serving time with their child maintained a parental relationship, even if it was with just one of their children; as a result, they were mentally and physically healthier than other inmates. They were not as heavily affected by depression or overwhelmed by guilt in contrast to those who did not have an opportunity to maintain their parental relationship. Most of the women were involved in drug abusing, drug dealing, or other criminal activities that had no place for children. Serving time with a child in prison gave them an opportunity to experience their children's day-to-day existence. It was also a turning point for mothers and turned their life upside down. They were thinking of finding a job, even low-status ones, to be able to keep their children upon being released.

I am ready to do housekeeping or even running public WCs to earn money. (Incarcerated woman, two years imprisoned)

I'm thinking I will get a job when I go out. I will do secretarial work or salesmanship. Although these may not be good jobs, that's enough to earn money enough for a baby. When I go out, I have a plan to live just like others. My entire hope is my kid. (Incarcerated woman, three years imprisoned)

They had an intention to step away from crime and return to their family support system rather than the prison or criminal network as well as to improve their familial relations. The benefits of a positive mother-child interaction in prison led them toward reuniting with family after a long-term separation. Although Maryam's husband was criminal and they got divorced, she reconsidered joining him and rebuilding a family because of her child.

I'm ready to live with my criminal husband only for the sake of my baby. I called my husband and said 'Let's live together. A boy is involved in our life.' (Incarcerated woman, two years imprisoned)

Mother-child interactions in prison significantly contributed to transforming and rehabilitating mothers. Almost all the mothers in my study used and dealt drugs. In addition to the familial dysfunction, divorce, addiction, and a lack of support, they were the primary breadwinner and caretaker of their children. Dealing drugs was among the most popular activities performed to earn money. However, the presence of children in prison keep them away from using or dealing drugs.

I don't whirl in the street for drugs anymore, I never think to use drugs. I embrace my baby and think about how much he is bothered by the smoke. I can't do this; he makes me stay away from drugs. (Incarcerated woman, two years imprisoned)

My kid helps me to not do any wrong in prison. I want to make my husband give up [drug misuse] for the sake of my baby. We want to live, even move from that neighborhood in which we did wrong, and I want to control myself and cut my relationships with all my deviant friends. This baby is my break. I feel bad about my baby. I'm responsible for my baby. (Incarcerated woman, three years imprisoned)

All in all, allowing incarcerated mothers to keep their children has numerous benefits for mothers who are going to encounter significant blocks of free time in prison. Not all incarcerated mothers had an opportunity to live in prison with their children for one reason or another. For those mothers, the effect of the separation is substantial. Most participants of this study lost their emotional bonds with their parents, which will be coupled with the disconnection from their children and increased levels of anxiety. Some of them were left with suicidal feelings, guilt, and depression, especially those who were the primary caregiver and breadwinner of their children.

> *I have seven children that are living in the south, and I was the only one who fed them. They are all under 10. How they can take care of themselves now? Since affording their life was so challenging for me, I decided to transfer drugs. The very first time I transferred drugs, I was arrested. That is it. I have not earned anything, and I'm locked up in prison. I'm on death row. I wanted to kill myself several times. I'm useless, I'm helpless. What's goanna happen to those innocents, to my children.* (Incarcerated woman, six years imprisoned)

The Most Visible Victims

It was a hot summer in 2012 when I saw Shirin, a three-year-old girl, hanging on her mother's chador in a prison in central Iran. She was among hundreds of incarcerated women of different ages and background as well as children of both sexes from infancy to five years old. The only people she knew were mothers and children in the mothers' ward, and she barely had communication with men. She was lucky to have an opportunity to attend the kindergarten that was located in the prison. She was extremely lucky that one non-governmental organization took responsibility for training teachers in the kindergarten and providing them with educational facilities. She was lucky enough to not be in the prison from 8 in the morning until 4 in the evening. She was lucky enough to be surrounded by other children in the mothers' cell. However, she was not lucky enough to have her mom's emotional support for the rest of her life, as her mother was on death row for murdering her husband in a drug-related fight three years ago. She was not lucky enough to be supported by her mother's family members since she was a result of extramarital sex of mother with a drug dealer, so none of the family members knew about her existence, as she was born in the prison. She was not lucky enough to be accepted by the grandparents or even aunts or uncles since her mother was a shame of the family. She was not lucky enough to be considered as a human who would need support after her mother's death. Even her grandparents, who recently learned about the grandchild in the prison, refused to even consider her as their own grandchild. They did offer help (i.e. hiring a professional and well-known lawyer) under the condition that she give up her child and send her to a governmental foster home or welfare center. She was not lucky enough to grow up among family members and not start her life behind closed doors and long walls. The only time she saw the blue sky was from the restricted, gray, long, narrow yards in the prison. She was still lucky to not be born 30 years ago, however, after the Islamic Revolution. Maryam, a baby girl born in prison right after the revolution among all material world just had an opportunity to see a hose that was always in the yard of the prison. Both were born in the scariest world possible.

In the middle of the mother's ward, there was a five-year-old girl whose mother was arrested when her father wanted to smuggle drugs from Kerman to afford their life. She was a mentally disabled. She caught my eyes in the overcrowded and noisy so-called mothers' cell. She raised her hands toward the sky and started praying. She could not speak properly, but it was an emotional experience to realize what she was praying for. She prayed for her freedom, and she asked to be taken back to their home with her siblings who were alone and waiting for the parent. Her siblings who were left outside did not even know where their parent has gone. They had just their parent who was now incarcerated.

A three-year-old boy with green eyes and blond hair was with his mother, who was sentenced to five years. He was the only boy among seven other girls on the ward. His mother was always fighting with other mothers to defend his rights in that small room. They had to sleep next to their mothers in the same bed, no matter how small it was. They had to manage to sleep in the tiny space. They were supposed to keep the air conditioner on during the summer, which made the situation frustrating for those children who were sleeping right in front of the air conditioner, as they were almost always cold and sick. It is difficult to simply discuss the child-mother interactions in prison in terms of being a protector of children or mothers. Or, it is difficult to simply say that children were the saviors of their incarcerated mothers. Or, it is hard to believe that the emotional bonds between mothers and children were temporary and represented a predicament for both of them in case of the mother's execution or having to give up the child to a family member, foster home, or welfare center.

As a researcher, I felt confused by conflicting directions, as my previous studies had focused on protecting children's rights and protecting children's interests on one side, incarcerated women's rehabilitation and reforming, and the pain of imprisonment for children on the other side. Although I did some of this research in 2012, I still have a sense that something wrong happened while writing this chapter in 2020. A part of this feeling is due to the lack of alternative programs such as GPS-monitored home detention, low-security prisons, releasing mothers who are primary caregivers, and mother-child residential facilities. Another part of this tension is related to the "pain of imprisonment" for children who are neglected and misused by the authorities. All disciplines and regulations to structure inmates' life in prison were applied to children as well including the bedtimes, mealtimes, television rules, cell rules, and so on.

Several studies have indicated that the physical environments of prisons in many countries, including South Africa, Romania, Venezuela, and Egypt, have not been designed to protect children's rights, or, it may be more accurate to say, they are not child-friendly (Whitman 1992; Cartner 1992; Mariner and Bochenek 1997; Van Hout and Gunda, 2019; Taylor 2004). According to Forooeddin et al. (2007), children who were in one of the prisons in Iran suffered from bodily injuries (e.g. bruises, contusions, abrasions, cheek scratches, and bruised lips), various kinds of infections (e.g. cervical, otitis, cerumen, pharyngitis), psychological trauma (e.g. mental retardation, incompatibility, aggressiveness, nail biting, or nocturnal enuresis), and showed poor performances in locomotion, socialization, and self-help.

Concerns and moral oppositions against keeping children with their mothers in prisons with limited mother-child welfare facilities are worthy of consideration. Do incarcerated mothers sacrifice or put aside their needs for their children's interests or vice versa? Is the physical closeness of a mother and child more fulfilling and gratifying for mothers or children? Although children and mothers are kept in a separate cell, they still communicate with a wide range of criminals in the shared yard. In the prison I visited, mother-child cells were called "*band-e madaran*" (mom's ward). Among the incarcerated women, children were running in the yard carelessly with absolutely no idea where they were playing and with whom they were communicating. The yard was small for the overcrowded women's ward, but it was still appreciated and cherished by the children as a place to have fun. They were affected by prison language from prison slang, the secret languages, and the argot. Inmates would tease and make fun of the children in the yard; it was one of the inmates' favorite forms of entertainment. Even children, however, were victims of physical and verbal abuse from inmates. Children were around when incarcerated women talked about their sexual relationships, criminal activities, sexual abuse, broken families, the devastated situation of their children outside the prison, and so on. Besides learning inappropriate words at early ages, fighting and violence among inmates became a part of children's games in the prison. When children fought, their mothers would fight as well to protect their children. Therefore, due to a lack of leisure facilities (e.g. toys) in an overcrowded cell where 23 mothers and children lived, fighting and cursing were inevitable.

> *Fighting is inevitable here, and bad talk is being spoken. I don't want my kid to learn bad habits.* (Incarcerated woman, three years imprisoned)
>
> *Out of this room, all people curse and talk dirty, I'm afraid my kid will learn that type of talking.* (Incarcerated woman, four years imprisoned)

Children were around when mothers initiated negotiations about their crimes and defended and justified their criminal activities among other inmates. One mother who was convicted of first-degree robbery justified her criminal activities while holding her son. *"At least I have not killed anyone, and at least I have never used drugs. I'm not that dirty."* In response, a mother in the next bunk bed who was convicted of first-degree murder while playing with her baby girl said, *"At least we did not climb up someone's wall. We have not stolen someone's property."*

Children were locked up in dark cell with limited space, a lack of sunlight, temperature imbalances, and proximity to the bathrooms increased their risk of getting infected by a wide variety of viruses. There was no time when a mother and child could have privacy, as there were always other inmates with their children present. To avoid the constant exposure to other inmates, they blocked their beds with sheets or chadors to give them some privacy so they could have one-on-one time with their children. However, guards protested against covering the beds with curtains, as this went against the visibility rules in prison to control sexual activities and drug abuse.

> *Nobody cares about our kids, and we should take care of them. When a mother or their kids get sick here in the cell, other kids get sick as well. And when they get sick, it is so difficult to take care of them since we live with 20 people, and they talk, they run, they eat, and they make noise. Even if your kid is sleeping and sick, you cannot ask everyone to keep down their voices. After all, it is prison. It is not the only problem that we have, as the air conditioner during the summer literally kills some kids. My bed is right in front of it, and my kids and I are always cold, and it takes a million years to get better since I am not allowed to turn it off, as other inmates would kill me.* (Incarcerated woman, three years imprisoned)

Also, the cell doors are all closed in the evening, and the mothers and children do not have access to fresh air from evening until the next morning. Although surveillance cameras were in all the cells, in a case of emergency, there was a possibility that the guards would not hear their voices or monitor the cameras.

> *One of the pregnant women in this room gave birth to her son right here on this floor with no facilities, doctors, or nurses. We were her nurse and doctor that*

damn night. She screamed, and we screamed, and everybody screamed. Kids cried, and mothers punched the door, but nobody helped us that night. It was her time, and her baby was coming, and we were alone. We all cried. Even other cells realized something was happening in our cell, and they started to scream and punch their cell doors to notify the guards. But, you know, no one came. She gave birth to her baby with the help of us. In the morning, the guards came and opened the door. Just like that, as if nothing had happened that night." (Incarcerated woman, four years imprisoned)

There was no play area for children in the prison; they had to stay on the unit with their mothers or run in the yard and potentially be exposed to various incidents. The only time during the day when children could get distance from the prison atmosphere was during the kindergarten time, from the morning to the afternoon. It was extremely challenging for mothers to convince their children to get out without their mother's companionship. They have been with them as long as they can remember, and the only one who has taken care of them is their mother. Additionally, they have not gone anywhere without their mothers, as even on visiting days, mothers and children were always together. Furthermore, a regular topic of discussion in the mom's ward was separation days from children and their potential future caregivers, especially for those who were on death row or those who did not have any family to take care of their children. It took a long time for most of them to feel safe and secure to leave their mother. At the end, if they could not convince their children, they sent them forcefully regardless of their crying and screaming.

My daughter, my sweet daughter realized that I'm going to give her up in the near future since I'm on death row. She witnessed all my mourning and worry. She is smart, and she has realized that something is going to happen very soon. She clung tightly to me, and I cannot even go to the bathroom. She gave me a hard time about going to the kindergarten. She reads the worry in my eyes. Even now, it is too hard for her to go to the kindergarten, but she has to, she has to. (Incarcerated woman, three years imprisoned)

Human exchanges are limited in the prison, except during in-person family and non-contact (through glass) visits. Being locked up in the restricted environment with incarcerated women and eight children left limited opportunities for them to explore the outside world. All they know about animals, cars, homes, family, siblings, and so on are limited to the toys and photos in the kindergarten. The only people who they were in constant contact with were guards, prisoners, and, luckily, the instructors in the kindergarten, almost all of whom were women. Their contact with men was limited to family visiting times or warden visits to the cells and prisoners.

> *My daughter was born in the prison. When she was one year and a half, once she started to recognize people around, she was screaming and crying during the family visit time. She hid and did not talk with anyone who came to visit me. She was shocked, I can say. She was extremely shocked.* (Incarcerated woman, three years imprisoned)

There were no nurses or babysitters in the prison to take care of newborn babies and infants during family visits, especially during non-contact visits. Non-contact visits took place in a small and closed area in which there was no space for children to walk or run. There were no accommodations for children during the non-contact visits. Mothers were helpless during the visits to the extent that one of them asked me to hold her newborn baby while she was talking with her family. As a result of the lack of childcare professionals and advocates, nobody watched the mothers' behaviors with their children. The only pressure on them was the gaze of other mothers on the unit and also the dominant discourse of motherhood in the prison atmosphere, which worked as a panopticon to regulate their relations with their children. Nevertheless, comparing children with each other in front of them was always a trigger for fighting between mothers.

> *She won't stop comparing kids together. Whatever her son does, she starts to show off or explain to other inmates. She was always like this. Sometimes we fight over our kids to prove which kid is better.* (Incarcerated woman, five years imprisoned)

Three walls of the room had triple bunk beds, and each bunk bed was for three family members. Mothers and children shared the beds. For children's safety, mothers preferred the first level of the beds, and the rest were occupied by pregnant women (pregnant women were kept in the moms' ward). Even pregnant women could not use the second and third levels of the beds in their six months of pregnancy. As a result of the growing number of women in prisons, more and more children and mothers slept on the floor, unless someone was released, and they could move to her bed.

> *My baby and I should sleep on the floor; I should be careful no one steps on my baby.* (Incarcerated woman, three years imprisoned)

Even if the children wanted to play on the unit with other children during the silent times (i.e. when all doors were closed), it was not safe due to the metal beds with sharp edges and the sleeping infants and pregnant women around. In addition, their movements and noises made most of the inmates unhappy and angry. Although the prison provided children with two set of clothes and dried food ingredients, they suffered from a lack of clothes and nutritious food, especially for those who did not have a deposit in their accounts or financial support from their family.

> *I don't know what do. He is a kid, and I cannot control him every minute to not make his clothes dirty. I should wash his clothes every day; otherwise, he won't have clothes to wear. Who do you think can bring clothes for him in the prison? Nobody. His dad is in prison as well, and his siblings cannot afford their own lives, let alone this kid.* (Incarcerated woman, four years imprisoned)

They could not ask the family for clothes or money to buy extra food for the children, as the family already struggled with poverty. Those who received financial support provided their children with different kinds of food, which was not the case for most of the mothers.

> *When a mother who has money buys food or fruit, my son, Ali, cries so hard that I have to hit him or bring him out of the room. Most of the time when I notice that mothers want to give food to their babies, I take Ali out to the yard so that I'm not forced to hit him.* (Incarcerated woman, one year imprisoned)

Mothers of children who were born in the prison were responsible for applying for a birth certificate for their children. There were no legal services in the prison to follow up on the matter for moms. Incarcerated mothers, as previously discussed, have been excluded and abandoned by their family members who were the only potential advocate to arrange legal procedures for getting a certificate. Yet, beyond that, some of the mothers were involved in a temporary marriage (*sighe*) for one year, and their marriage certificates were expired as well. Mothers did not even have a chance to visit their so-called husband anymore to discuss the issue and ask for assistance.

> *My son, Hussein, is three years old now. His father was an Afghan, and I had a short-term marriage, Sigheh, with him, though all my family disagreed. Our marriage contract, Sigheh, expired a long time ago. No one wants this baby. Everybody is opposed. No one goes to get his identity certificate, and if we get the certificate the place of his father's name would be blank, since the duration of my Sigheh has ended, and my husband is not here to follow the certificate affairs.* (Incarcerated woman, three years imprisoned)

Being Prisoned Outside of Prison

Almost all mothers heard from the caregivers that their children experienced grief and anger. Children expressed their grief through non-stop crying, feeling lonely, and having nightmares. They experienced guilt, anxiety, depression, and stress. Mothers in the prison struggled to parent from a distance, and children outside the prison experienced a constant shifting of caregivers, a lack of food, school problems, health care issues, and poverty. A four-year-old boy of one of the participants who was living with his grandmother suffered from extreme behavioral and emotional issues due to his mother's incarceration.

> *Hossein has become so nervous. He constantly pairs my slippers at home. He doesn't let anyone use them. He takes care of my clothes. As soon as someone enters my room, he starts crying, screaming, and bawling. He doesn't sleep well at nights; suddenly, he wakes up and screams. He was taken to the doctor, and*

> *the doctor has prescribed a tranquilizer. My mother says he sleeps more calmly when he takes the medicine.* (Incarcerated woman, three years imprisoned)

Before their mothers' incarceration, almost all the children were exposed to life stressors such as parental drug abuse, parental mental illness, parents being involved in criminal activities, child abuse and neglect, disruptive family members, divorce, and poverty. The incarceration of the mothers intensified and exacerbated their pre-existing situation. Children might choose different escape strategies such as committing suicide, abusing drugs, and running away from home to deal with the enduring trauma of their mother's incarceration. Incarcerated mothers were the primary caregivers and breadwinners of the children, and almost all them were involved in drug dealing or drug abusing. Upon their arrest, children who were already being familiar with the drugs and the customers of their mother found the most available strategy for dealing with the tragedy. One of the participants who was one of the most popular drug dealers in the north of Isfahan had four children. She was a single parent and was the principal breadwinner of the family. Once she was incarcerated, she lost control over her children's lives, which left them with her addicted customers. Her two daughters became addicted to heroin in the absence of their mother.

> *Once they arrested me, I knew that something bad would happen to my children. I was a drug dealer, and my place was always full of addicts. I was in prison, and I heard that one of my daughters, who was 14 years old, started using heroin and sleeping with one of my customers. I beg the staff to help me out to at least save the rest of my children. I was in prison, and one day I heard that my older daughter, who was 17, got married to a drug dealer and was addicted to heroin. I had just two more children who are less than 10 years old. I know they are not doing well with the addicted sisters and customers.* (Incarcerated woman, two years imprisoned)

The unsecured life with the addicted father caused the 13-year-old girl to suffer to the extent that she attempted to kill herself three times. She was supposed to treat her father's friends, who were all addicted, with respect and prepare arrangements for them to use drugs. She was also responsible for facilitating the daily drug use of her father.

> *My daughter is mostly with her father. My husband is an addict. Every day, he brings home some of his friends. He has burned my daughter's hand several times. He punishes her. He tells her to go and buy drugs for him. My daughter has attempted suicide three times.* (Incarcerated woman, three years imprisoned)

A considerable number of children of incarcerated mothers escaped from their home after their mothers were arrested. Shahnaz was a mother with four children outside prison. She was one of the mothers who could not leave the social workers' office in the prison. There were two social workers inside the prison. Prisoners believed they could not assist them since they did not have power, or if they had power they would not help them. As a result, not all mothers relied on their assistance; however, some of them, like Shahnaz, who lost her children one after another, constantly begged them and cried for support. I was at one of her meetings with the social workers, and she even asked me to meet the children and help them. She asked the social workers to investigate her family's condition if they did not believe her. She provided them with her home address and phone number to collect the necessary information to support her. One of the social workers said, "*She has been here in this office every single day since she got arrested. She won't stop crying and telling her kids' stories.*" She had a twin who escaped from home. One of the twins got married and called her mother in the prison to announce her marriage.

> *I have 16-year-old twins, Leyla and Hasan. Leyla escaped from home last month. She quit her studies, and then she informed us that she's married. After that, Hasan's also escaped from home and quit his studies. He hasn't come back anymore, but he has informed us that he's busy working.* (Incarcerated woman, two years imprisoned)

Some believe that the children are better off in the prison than in the outside world, as they at least have a safe and secure place to sleep and food to eat. Children who have been left behind the walls lived with extended kin who have been already overwhelmed by the financial issues of their own children, welfare organizations, or fathers who were probably addicts, financially unstable, and criminals. However, neither of them were particularly good caregiving options for the children of incarcerated mothers. Being loved and accepted among a semblance of family and having strong bonds and ties with an alternative caregiver are crucial to the child's development. In a situation in which fathers and grandparents were not able to take care of children, some other relatives showed a willingness to accept the responsibility. When possible, mothers preferred to leave children with the relative-caregivers so they could be in a familiar, safe, and stable environment; otherwise, the last option that almost all mothers and children did their best to avoid was relying on welfare organizations due to the risk of losing connections with siblings, extended family, friends, and the community. However, since almost all kinship caregivers struggled with financial issues, children either passed from caregiver to caregiver and experienced several moves or were separated from their siblings. No financial assistance from the government was available for the caregivers who were involved in raising the children. In the absence of the family caregivers, older siblings could take care of the rest to prevent the siblings' separation. Nevertheless, it is the only option for some families without alternative caregivers or due to a large number of children making it financially impossible to take care of all of them.

It is expected that children with fathers and kin caregivers feel more love and safety than those who are in welfare institutions. Also, caregivers were expected to facilitate mother-child visitations more often than the foster care organizations. Alternative caregivers of children in my study were all either old, impoverished, uneducated, addicted, criminals, and so on. Children of incarcerated mothers were in limbo; they had neither a way to become free from the indecent caregivers nor adjust to their new so-called family. The children of one participant left with their father, who was addicted to methamphetamine and involved in criminal activities (i.e. drug dealing). The mother has always been an emotional and physical protector of the children from their addicted father. Also, she protected her young girl from the addicts and criminals in the community. Being afraid of the father was not the only issue for her 17-year-old daughter, as living in a high-crime neighborhood kept her alert and nervous all day and night.

> *My three children are with my husband. My child says, 'Mama! Papa smokes glass narcotics; he's sitting behind us with a knife from night to morning. We can't sleep. We're scared. He's locked the door. We're afraid that he'll kill us. Mama, we're scared from night to morning.' My elder daughter says, 'Papa isn't home. My siblings go to school. I'm alone at home. Many punks are on the roof and in the lane. I'm afraid that they will rush into the house and hurt me.'* (Incarcerated woman, one year imprisoned)

No policies or programs addressed, monitored, supervised, or scrutinized the circumstances and needs of children who were with kinship caregivers, which was the only chance for mothers to keep children inside the family instead of sending them out to welfare institutions. However, some caregivers suffered from long-term physiological and physical impairments and illnesses, which negatively impacted the children's healthy development. A participant's son lived with a sister-in-law who was in mental and psychological critical condition due to the loss of her baby. She tried by all means to take him away from her and give him to her mom; however, there were no legal services in the prison to help her resolve the issue. The family of her husband took the child away from the family of the mother, as once they realized she was incarcerated, they were not willing to give him to the grandmother.

> *Nobody helps me. They've given my child to a woman who is severely depressed and just shouts and cries because of her child's death. She constantly takes narcotics and drugs. I'm scared. What's happening to my child?! I can't do anything. They don't let my mother take my child. My child's perishing there.* (Incarcerated woman, one year imprisoned)

Older children acting as a caregiver of siblings is another option for those whom their mothers were a primary caregiver. Older children play a role as parent for the rest, which means they often have to drop out of school for the sake of family and become a child laborer to afford family expenses. Mojgan's daughter took a job as a secretary for physicians to financially assist her mother before her incarceration. However, she was forced to quit the job and school to care for her siblings in the absence of her mother.

> *My elder daughter is only 17 and has quit her studies. She was a doctors' secretary, but she quit that, too. She takes care of three other children. She has no other income. My daughter says, 'Mama, the children don't listen to me. They are so annoying. I can't protect three children alone. I can't even step away from the children anymore; I'm afraid that they will get hurt. I've quit school and my job, mama. My brother doesn't listen to me at all; he doesn't obey me at all.'* (Incarcerated woman, two years imprisoned)

Although maintaining mother-child contact during incarceration can have benefits for both children and mothers, the barriers to more frequent contact, including child-unfriendly facilities, the cost of maintaining contact, strained mother-caregiver relationships, and welfare institutions' policies, were substantial. Children of incarcerated mothers could maintain their connections through three methods: in-person visits, cabin visits, and telephone calls.

One of the most popular communication methods between mothers and children was in-person visits. Mothers went through a dark, narrow, and gray corridor before entering a visiting area. Once all the visitors came to the visiting area, a small door was opened by a woman guard, and incarcerated women with a more or less same color chador came outside and searched for their family members. A big yard in an open area, which was sectioned by metal bars with a metal ceiling, was allocated for in-person visits. Strangely enough, there was a playground with recreational facilities (e.g. swings and slides) for the children at the back of the yard. However, mothers and children who did not have a chance to regularly visit preferred to spend all 40 minutes with each other. Some families distracted children after in-person visitations by giving them a break to play in the playground with other children. Visitors and mothers sat on a floor covered by carpet. They ate food, talked about their lives, cried, played with their children, exchanged some gifts, and so on. When it came for the separation time, the children could not stop crying and begging their mothers to stay with them. There was a boy around eight years old who followed his mom until they reached the gray small door of the women's unit. His mother could not look at him, and she tried to hide her eyes full of tears from the boy by her chador. When the mother entered the corridor and he could not see her any more, he started to beg:

> *Mom, mom, for the sake of god, come back, mom. I won't go home without you, I won't go, I swear to God, I won't go. I will stay here overnight.* (Incarcerated woman, two years imprisoned)
>
> Or, as one of the mothers stated: *"When my 13-year-old son comes for a face-to-face visit, he can't get back and says, 'Mama, for god's sake, stay five minutes more; mama, stay for me.' My child begs me; he doesn't separate. I'm always the last person to get back to the prison. He accompanies me to the exit door and says, 'Mama, don't go inside. The hallway is so dark, tall, and horrible.' My child always asks, 'Mama, is the prison the same? Aren't you scared?' My child is scared himself. When he sees the atmosphere, he gets more anxious."* (Incarcerated woman, three years imprisoned)

Maintaining in-person visits with children was challenging due to the travel distance and a lack of transportation. Most of the children did not have the resources (e.g. money and transportation) to visit their mothers in person.

> *I see my children every eight months, and each time I see just two of them. Because it's difficult for them to come from our city; it's so far, and it costs a lot. They have to leave our city two days before the time of visit, and immediately after that, they go back exhausted. It's so hard for them to travel this far distance just for a 40-minute visit. When they have to get separated, they beg me not to go. They all get sick when they leave me. They want to sleep a night with me. They want to stay in my bosom for hours. But, the time of the visit is so short; I wish it were at least longer, or at least I was in my own city.* (Incarcerated woman, five years imprisoned)

Even if they had resources, caregivers were gatekeepers who might be unwilling to expose children to the child-unfriendly environment in the prison. The visiting room, especially for cabin visits, was frightening and traumatic for children. Besides waiting in a long line in a small, dirty, and crowded waiting room for hours, they were exposed to indecent treatment of corrections staff. The waiting room for visitors in the prison I studied was overcrowded and left no space for children to move or run, and all were frustrated and overwhelmed. In addition, the strained relationships between mothers and caregivers played a crucial role in the frequency of visitations, and most mothers were excluded from the family. As a result, caregivers did their best to prevent mother-child visitations with the hope that the child would forget the mother one day.

> *They were thinking that if my daughter does not see me, she will be much happier. They were thinking that our visitations would harm a child. They said, 'It is better for her to forget her addicted mother'. They said, 'If you loved your kid, you never would have gone to prison'. They said, 'You do not have a heart, better that your kid forgets you.'* (Incarcerated woman, two years imprisoned)

The possibility of communication was largely dependent on the child's age as well. Children under seven were not willing to talk on the phone with their mothers, which left them with just one method of communication: in-person visits. They were not even interested in talking over the phone in a cabin visit. Corrections staff and guards were in every corner of the cabin visit, and the gray walls and metal cabins were not child-friendly at all. Almost all children who were around three to seven were upset and frightened during the cabin visits. Mothers cried since they could not hug and calm their children. The caregivers were all overwhelmed, frustrated, and confused, since they were helpless to manage the situation where the mothers begged the children to talk, and they were denied. Most of the children hid in a crowd or sat on the floor and cried.

> *Whenever she came here to visit me, she would sit on the floor far from the cabins and cry. She even turned her eyes from me. She tried to hide between her arms. Every time I cried and begged her. My mom, who is her caregiver, begs her to talk with me, but she never does that. Here, it is noisy and depressing and scary, I know, but I want her. What can I do? I cannot leave without seeing her."* (Incarcerated woman, two years imprisoned)

For school-age children, telephone contact was challenging since mothers had limited times during the week and were locked in their units when children came back from school. Even if they could talk with their children, the duration would not last more than three to five minutes each time, and this communication had to be managed by not only family members, but also a lawyer (if any) and plaintiffs.

> *I don't know with whom I could talk with my 17-year-old daughter or my plaintiffs or caregivers. With my daughter, who always cries when she hears my voice over the phone, it takes minutes for her to put herself together and listen to me. She just begs and cries. I much prefer to talk to her for all the three or five minutes, but I cannot, as I have to talk with the plaintiffs as well.* (Incarcerated woman, three years imprisoned)

The methadone maintenance treatment (MMT) and presence of children in Iranian prisons keep the bodies and spirits of prisoners controllable and dependable. Neither the MMT nor the life of children in prison is based on treatment or rehabilitation programs, and neither are followed by supporting educational programs. Surprisingly, both are found to be remarkable resources for controlling and monitoring prisoners. The roots of these two techniques of power in prison can hardly be found in a particular plan or scientific knowledge; rather, both became permanent programs inside the prisons simultaneously and rather incidentally. After monitoring the impact of the MMT and the presence of children on prisoners, even with a lack of educational and training programs and poor care after release from prison, they were deemed as beneficial for the total institution.

Drugs and children in prison complement torture as a technique that produces an extreme degree of pain for prisoners and their family members. The continuous endurance of the physical punishment of prisoners and their family members in Iran is a demonstration of how the power really operates in this country. It takes both manifest and more hidden forms. Torture and public executions refer to the former. As to the latter, public spectacles in the prison yard and visiting rooms are occasionally offered for prisoners and their family members. Among the scenes described to me were an incarcerated mother appearing in a prison yard grief-ravaged and distraught, begging guards to help her children outside the prison; an incarcerated mother on death row with her child clinging to her leg going through the exit door to become apart for ever; a mother crying and scratching the glass window during a cabin visit to touch her child; drug abusers going through painful days of detoxification by themselves in a corner of the prison yard without any clinical support; prisoners fighting in a methadone line to get their dose sooner; and prisoners begging for a higher dose from the guards in front of all the other prisoners. Although those scenes were not public executions, they are still a great alternative spectacle of physical punishment and unbearable pain.

References

Anaraki, N. R., & Boostani, D. (2014a). Living in and Living Out: A Qualitative Study of Incarcerated Mothers' Narratives of Their Children's Living Condition. *Quality & Quantity, 48*(6), 3093–3107.

Anaraki, N. R., & Boostani, D. (2014b). Mother-Child Interaction: A Qualitative Investigation of Imprisoned Mothers. *Quality & Quantity, 48*(5), 2447–2461.

Baunach, P. J. (1985). *Mothers in Prison*. New Jersey: Transaction Books.

Beaver, K. M., & Wright, J. P. (2007). A Child Effects Explanation for the Association Between Family Risk and Involvement in an Antisocial Lifestyle. *Journal Of Adolescent Research, 22*(6), 640–664.

Belknap, J., & Holsinger, K. (2006). The Gendered Nature of Risk Factors for Delinquency. *Feminist Criminol, 1*, 48–71.

Bowlby, J. (1952). *Maternal Care and Mental Health*. Geneva: World Health Organization.

Brennan, T., Breitenbach, M., Dieterich, W., Salisbury, E. J., & Voorhis, P. V. (2012). Women's Pathways to Serious and Habitual Crime: A Person-Centered Analysis Incorporating Gender Responsive Factors. *Crim. Justice Behav, 39*(11), 1481–1508.

Calhoun, G. B. (2001). Differences Between Male and Female Juvenile Offenders as Measured by the BASC. *Journal of Offender Rehabilitation, 33*, 87–96.

Cartner, H. (1992). Prison Conditions in Romania. Human Rights Watch.

Catan, L. (1992). Infants with Mothers in Prison. In R. Shaw (Ed.), *Prisoners' Children, What Are the Issues?* London: Routledge.
Celinska, K., & Siegel, J. A. (2010). Mothers in Trouble: Coping with Actual or Pending Separation from Children Due to Incarceration. *Prison J., 90*, 447–474.
Covington, S. S. (1998). Women in Prison: Approaches in the Treatment of Our Most Invisible Population. *Women Therapy, 21*(1), 141–155.
Covington, S. S. (2002). A Woman's Journey Home: Challenges for Female Offenders and Their Children. In: "From Prison To Home" Conference. US Department of Health and Human Services and the Urban Institute, Washington.
Cunningham, A. (2001). Forgotten Families—The Impacts of Imprisonment. *Fam. Matters, 59*, 35.
Dalley, L. P. (2002). Policy Implications Relating to Inmate Mothers and Their Children: Will the Past Be Prologue? *The Prison Journal, 82*(2), 234–268.
Daly, K. (1992). Women's Pathways to Felony Court: Feminist Theories of Lawbreaking and Problems of Representation. *S. Cal. Rev. L. & Women's Stud, 2*, 11.
Defina, R. H., & Hannon, L. (2010). The Impact of Adult Incarceration on Child Poverty: A County-Level Analysis, 1995-2007. *The Prison Journal, 90*(4), 377–396.
Dehart, D. D. (2008). Pathways to Prison: Impact of Victimization in the Lives of Incarcerated Women. *Violence Against Women, 14*, 1362–1381.
Eddy, J. M., & Reid, J. B. (2002). The Antisocial Behavior of the Adolescent Children of Incarcerated Parents: A Developmental Perspective. Paper Presented at the From Prison to Home Conference, Washington, DC.
Eloff, I., & Moen, M. (2010). An Analysis of Mother–Child Interaction Patterns in Prison. *Early Child Dev. Care, 173*(6), 711–720.
Ferrara, P., Emmanuele, V., Nicoletti, A., Mastrangelo, A., Marrone, G., & Pedote, G. (2007). Mothers with Their Babies in Prison: The First Italian Experience. *Arch. Dis. Child., 92*(2), 183.
Flynn, C. (2012). Caring for the Children of Imprisoned Mothers: Exploring the Role of Fathers. *Child Abuse. Rev., 21*(4), 285–298.
Fontaine, N., Carbonneau, R., Vitaro, F., Barker, E. D., & Tremblay, R. E. (2009). A Critical Review of Studies on the Developmental Trajectories of Antisocial Behavior in Females. *J. Child Psychol. Psychiatry, 50*, 363–385.

Forooeddin, A., Biglarian, A., & Dadkhah, A. (2007). Physical and Social Circumstances of Children in Iran Affected by the Incarceration of the Mother. *Int. J. Soc. Welf., 16*(3), 278–280.

Foster, H., & Hagan, J. (2007). Incarceration and Intergenerational Social Exclusion. *Soc. Probl., 54*, 399–433.

Franklin, C. (2008). Women Offenders, Disparate Treatment, and Criminal Justice a Theoretical, Historical, and Contemporary Overview. *Crim. Justice Stud., 21*, 341–360.

Fritsch, T., & Burkhead, J. (1981). Behavioral Reactions of Children to Parental Absence Due to Imprisonment. *Fam. Relat., 3*(1), 83–88.

Green, B. L., Miranda, J., Daroowalla, A., & Siddique, J. (2005). Trauma Exposure, Mental Health Functioning and Program Needs of Women in Jail. *Crime Delinq, 51*, 133–151.

Hagan, J., & Dinovitzer, R. (1999). Collateral Consequences of Imprisonment for Children, Communities, and Prisoners. *Crime and Justice, 26*, 121–162.

Harden, J., & Hill, M. (1998). *Breaking the Rules: Women in Prison and Feminist Therapy*. New York: Harrington Park Press.

Hartz-Karp, J. (1983). The Impact of Infants in Prison on Institutional Life: A Study of the Mother-Infant Prison Programme in Western Australia Australian and New Zealand. *Aust. N. Z. J. Criminol, 16*(3), 172–183.

Hissel, S., Bijleveld, C., & Kruttschnitt, C. (2011). The Well-Being of Children of Incarcerated Mothers: An Exploratory Study for the Netherlands. *Eur. J. Criminol, 8*(5), 346–360.

Holsinger, K., & Holsinger, A. M. (2005). Differential Pathways to Violence and Self-Injurious Behavior: African American and White Girls in the Juvenile Justice System. *Journal of Research in Crime and Delinquency, 42*(2), 211–242.

Hungerford, G. (1993). The Children of Inmate Mothers: An Exploratory Study of Children, Caretakers and Inmate Mothers in Ohio. PhD Thesis, The Ohio State University.

Javdani, S., Sadeh, N., & Verona, E. (2011). Expanding Our Lens: Female Pathways to Antisocial Behavior in Adolescence and Adulthood. *Clinical Psychology Review, 31*(8), 1324–1348.

Johnson, R. (2009). Ever-Increasing Levels of Parental Incarceration and the Consequences for Children. Do Prisons Make Us Safer? The Benefits and Costs of the Prison Boom, 177–206.

Johnson, E. I., & Waldfogel, J. (2002). Parental Incarceration: Recent Trends and Implications for Child Welfare. *Social Service Review, 76*(3), 460–479.

Juliette, P. (2008). *Alternatives to Incarceration for Non-Violent Female Felony Offenders in New York State*. New York: State University of New York Empire State College.

Kochal, R., & Shamai, M. (2008). Motherhood Starts in Prison: The Experience of Motherhood Among Women in Prison. *Fam. Process, 47*(3), 323–340.

Kruttschnitt, C., & Gartner, R. (2003). Women's Imprisonment. *Crime Justice, 30*, 1–81.

Macbride, R. L. (2008). Incarcerated Mothers in Cuenca, Ecuador: Perceptions of Their Environment and the Impact It Has on the Lives of Their Young Children and Their Education. PhD Dissertation, University Of North Texas.

Maghsoudi, A., Anaraki, N. R., & Boostani, D. (2018). Patriarchy as a Contextual and Gendered Pathway to Crime: A Qualitative Study of Iranian Women Offenders. *Quality & Quantity, 52*(1), 355–370.

Makarios, M. D. (2007). Race, Abuse, and Female Criminal Violence. *Feminist Criminol., 2*, 100–116.

Mariner, J., & Bochenek, M. (1997). *Venezuela—Punishment Before Trial: Prison Conditions in Venezuela*. New York: Human Right Watch/Americas.

Mcdaniels-Wilson, C., & Belknap, J. (2008). The Extensive Sexual Violation and Sexual Abuse Histories of Incarcerated Women. *Violence Against Women, 14*(10), 1090–1127.

Miller, E. (1986). *Street Women*. Philadelphia: Temple University Press.

Moffitt, T. E. (1993). The Neuropsychology of Conduct Disorder. *Dev. Psychopathol., 5*, 135–152.

Molaverdi, Sh. (2015). Two hundred children accompanying mothers in prison, Islamic Republic News Agency, published Tuesday, May 5, 2015.

Mumola, C. J. (2000). *Incarcerated Parents and Their Children*. Washington DC: U.S. Department Of Justice, Bureau of Justice Statistics, Special Report.

Murray, J., Farrington, D. P., Sekol, I., & Olsen, R. F. (2009). Effects of Parental Imprisonment on Child Antisocial Behaviour and Mental Health: A Systematic Review. *Campbell Systematic Reviews, 5*(1), 1–105.

Owen, B., & Bloom, B. (2000). *Profiling the Needs of Young Female Offenders: Instrument Development And Pilot Study—Final Report*. Washington: U.S. Department of Justice.

Parke, R., & Clarke-Stewart, K. A. (2002). Effects of Parental Incarceration on Young Children. Presented at the Conference of "From Prison to Home", U.S. Department of Health and Human Services, The Urban Institute, January 30–31.

Poehlmann, J. (2005). Children's Family Environments and Intellectual Outcomes During Maternal Incarceration. *Journal of Marriage and Family, 67*(5), 1275–1285.
Pösö, T., Enroos, R., & Vierula, T. (2010). Children Residing in Prison with Their Parents: An Example of Institutional Invisibility. *The Prison Journal, 90*(4), 516–533.
Richie, B. E. (1996). *Compelled to Crime: The Gender Entrapment of Battered Black Women*. New York: Routledge.
Richie, B. (2001). Challenges Incarcerated Women Face as They Return to Their Communities: Findings from Life History Reviews. *Crime Delinq, 47*, 368–389.
Robertson, O. (2007). *The Impact of Parental Imprisonment on Children*. Geneva: Quaker United Nations Office.
Salisbury, E. J., & Van Voorhis, P. (2009). Gendered Pathways: An Empirical Investigation of Women Probationers' Paths to Incarceration. *Crim. Justice Behav., 36*, 541–566.
Scharff-Smith, P., & Gampell, L. (2011). *Children of Imprisoned Parents. European Network for Children of Imprisoned Parents*. Denmark: University of Ulster and Bambinisenzasbarre, The Danish Institute for Human Rights.
Seymour, C. (1998). Children with Parents in Prison: Child Welfare Policy, Program, and Practice Issues. *Child Welf, 77*(5), 469–493.
Sharpe, G. (2013). *Offending Girls: Young Women and Youth Justice*. London: Routledge.
Shechory, M., Perry, G., & Addad, M. (2011). Pathways to Women's Crime: Differences Among Women Convicted of Drug, Violence and Fraud Offenses. *J. Soc. Psychol., 151*(4), 399–416.
Simpson, S. S. (1989). Feminist Theory, Crime, and Justice. *Criminology, 27*(4), 605–632.
Simpson, S. S., Yahner, J. L., & Dugan, L. (2008). Understanding Women's Pathways to Jail: Analysing The Lives of Incarcerated Women. *Australian & New Zealand Journal of Criminology, 41*(1), 84–108.
Socorro, M. (2009). Mother–Child Relationships: Females Behind Bars and Their Children. MS Dissertation, The Department Of Criminal Justice California State University, Long Beach.
Steele, M.(2008). Attachment, actual experience and mental representation. In: Green, V. (ed.) Emotional Development in Psychoanalysis, Attachment Theory and Neuroscience: Creating Connections, pp 86–106. Routledge, London.
Taylor, R. (2004). Women in Prison. The Quaker United Nations Offices.

Van Hout, M. C., & Mhlanga-Gunda, R. (2019). 'Mankind Owes to the Child the Best That It Has to Give': Prison Conditions and the Health Situation and Rights of Children Incarcerated with Their Mothers in Sub-Saharan African Prisons. *BMC International Health and Human Rights, 19*(1), 13.

Villanueva, C., & Byrne, M. W. (2009). Mothers, Infants and Imprisonment: An Overview of Prison Nurseries and Community-Based Alternatives. Paper Presented at the Annual Meeting of the ASC Annual Meeting, Philadelphia Marriott Downtown, Philadelphia. http://Citation.Allacademic.Com/Meta/P380026_Index.Html.

Whitman, L. (1992). Children in Northern Ireland: Abused by Security Forces and Paramilitaries (Vol. 1245). Human Rights Watch.

Willis, K., & Rushforth, C. (2003). The Female Criminal: An Overview of Women's Drug Use and Offending Behaviour. *Trends & Issues in Crime and Criminal Justice, 264*, 1.

Wong, S. K. (2011). Reciprocal Effects of Family Disruption and Crime: A Panel Study of Canadian Municipalities. *West. Criminal. Rev, 12*(1), 43–63.

World Prison Brief. (2018). Institute for Crime & Justice Policy Research.

Zhang, K. C., Choo, A., & Lim, L. (2009). Interventions with Young Female Offenders and Teenage Girls at Risk: Alternative Educational Services in a Singapore Girls' Home. *Support Learn, 24*(3), 137–143.

5

Conclusion: Never Accomplished Modernization

The insight of Michel Foucault regarding the three forms of penal order is a useful point of departure when depicting the current state of Iranian prisons as well as the evolution of the penal system in this country over the last decades. Foucault starts his study of penal history by describing how the dominant legal system from the Middle Ages until the eighteenth century was centered on the human body and operated through corporal punishment and public executions. In an archaic form of the penal order, the body was the principal target of punishment and power was exercised through torture. However, from the eighteenth century on, European societies gradually moved away from physical violence and corporal punishment to embrace softer and less visible techniques and forms of control. They transitioned from punishing the body to punishing the soul.

The modern forms of power and control, which have seen a transition from scaffold to prison and from punishment to correction, rely on "detailed knowledge, routine intervention, and gentle correction" (Garland 1986, p. 851). In the modern penal technology, experts start to play a key role in the judicial process by forming knowledge of crime, recognizing abnormalities, and guiding toward correction. To be more

N. R. Anaraki, *Prison in Iran*, Palgrave Studies in Prisons and Penology,
https://doi.org/10.1007/978-3-030-57169-6_5

specific, the modern system of control regulates, improves, and transforms individuals instead of repressing, destroying, and dispensing of them. Although controlling the human body has long been the ultimate goal of penal institutions, in the modern system, the bodies are trained to be docile and obedient. Prisoners' bodies internalize training and are transformed into "self-controlled" ones, which has a direct effect on the "soul" and guides the behaviors and acts of individuals. "These methods, which made possible the meticulous control of the operations of the body, which assured the constant subjection of its forces and imposed upon them a relation of docility-utility, might be called 'disciplines'" (Foucault 1979, p. 137). To reach this point, the human as an object needs to be monitored, studied, and analyzed with the aim of gaining a degree of understanding of "its forces, its reactions, its strengths and weaknesses, its possibilities" (Garland 1986, p. 853). The more knowledge gained, the more controllable humans are, which constitutes the essence of the "power-knowledge" link unveiled by Foucault. Correctionalist regimes in the modern penal system provide individuals with pre-planned, well-developed, knowledge-based programs aimed at individual transformation through the "body" followed by the "soul." As Foucault (1979, p. 233) observes, the double foundation of prisons, the "juridico-economic" and "technico-disciplinary," which cover both the deprivation of liberty and individual transformation, makes it a "civilized" form of penalty.

However, in addition to "law" (crime and punishment) in the Middle Ages and "discipline" in the early modern times, Foucault also speaks of a more recent technique of exercising power, "security." Power as security is exercised over the entire population rather than within the borders of a territory or over the bodies of individuals to "improve the condition of the population, to increase its wealth, its longevity, and its health" through "acting directly on the population itself through campaigns, or, indirectly, by, for example, techniques that, without people being aware of it, stimulate the birth rate, or direct the flows of population to this or that region or activity" (Foucault 2007, p. 105). The main issue of this new art of government is maintaining and developing dynamic forces, which has been called the "mechanism of security." Two techniques or technological assemblages underpin security: (1) the military-diplomatic, which consists of double instrumentations—"the multilateral diplomacy" and "the professional army"; and (2) the police, which involves the number of men, necessities of life, problems of health, activities of the population, and circulation of goods. In the new art of governance, concerns go beyond just living, as "doing better than just living, coexisting, and communicating can in fact be converted into forces of the state" (Foucault 2007, p. 327). The five key elements of the new governmentality are the naturalness of the society, the coexistence of science and decision making, the state taking responsibility for the population, the reliance on the natural economic and demographic processes, and the integration of freedom. As Foucault (2007, p. 354) states, the new governmentality "has to refer to the economy as a domain of naturalness: it has to manage populations; it also has to organize a legal system of respect for freedoms; and finally it has to provide itself with an instrument of direct, but negative, intervention, which is the police."

Sovereignty as the ultimate expression of law, discipline, and security (governmentality) co-exists and complements each other in most cases. However, in the Iranian case the first mechanism continues to dominate and to a significant extent substitute the other two. The outcomes of the study presented in this book suggest that the exercise of power through physical punishment constitutes a distinctive feature of the Iranian penal system. This conclusion applies both to torture as such and to prison as a supposedly distinctive institution.

This book has analyzed how prisoners and their families, particularly their children, have been governed and monitored not through various sorts of expert knowledge, but rather through the tortured bodies and spirits. In contrast to Foucault's (1979, p. 8) assertion that "the body as the major target of penal repression disappeared," this book revealed that patterns in the control of prisoners in both the past and the present in Iran have relied on the body. Foucault associated the transformation or progressive disappearance of "the gloomy festival of punishment" with the raise of modernity. Punishment as a spectacle or ceremony disappeared by the end of the eighteenth and the beginning of nineteenth century in Europe, and it became a hidden part of the penal system, followed by the bodiless reality.

However, both punishment and prison co-exist and complement one another in Iran. How could we possibly accept the claim that the body and pain are not the ultimate targets of punitive action, while prisoners are managed through smuggled drugs and methadone, by making incarcerated women powerless and frustrated in their attempts to provide for the children inside and outside the prisons, or by targeting the children as a means of exercising power?

One will end up on a wrong path if, when trying to make sense of the Iranian penal system he or she chooses to rely on the concept of power-knowledge "as a set of developing relationships between power, knowledge, and the body" or "an art of the body" as a framework of this country's penal history (Foucault 1979, p. 137). It would be particularly deceptive to consider the current inadequate training-based prison programs as a manifestation of the "science of man" (Garland 1986, p. 853). The body continues to be the principal target of the penal system in Iran. The body is not manipulated for higher aims (i.e. individual transformation, reformation, and correction) nevertheless, probably except for a short period of time right after the Islamic Revolution, when an attempt to Islamize prisoners by controlling and managing their bodies through applying pain was made.

According to Foucault, as societies have become more disciplinary, torture is no longer a principal means of government or a technique for exercising power. The aim of punishment is not anymore to take revenge on criminals, cause criminals to suffer, or put their pain on display, but to transform criminals, change their spirit, and prevent future crimes. However, poorly equipped and unsuitable rehabilitation programs in Iranian prisons cannot heal the delinquent past of prisoners, cannot remedy the problem of poverty that their children face, cannot deal with prisoners' long history of drug abuse and addiction, cannot remedy the child-mother separation, and cannot address the lack of essential necessities in prisons and outside of them.

The entry of children into the "equation" of discipline deserves particular attention. The point here is not to discourage the children's presence in prisons, but instead to argue for a fuller understanding of the effect of imprisonment on them, whether in prison or outside, and to highlight the prevalence of torturing the bodies of both mothers and their children. The argument made in this book is not that the children's presence in prisons is cruel, but rather that women prisoners are controlled by the penitentiary administration through their children. While some positive attempts such as establishing a kindergarten in a prison have been made to lessen the pain of imprisonment for the children, few prisons have implemented this measure. While the establishment of kindergartens cannot be ignored, it does not suffice to exempt the children from the severe pains of imprisonment.

The book does not say much about the systematic torture against political activists in different periods of Iran's history. Much has already been written on the subject of the torture of political prisoners (Abrahamian 1999), and although it is impossible to ignore this issue when studying prisons in Iran, my intention was to explore and depict the pains of living in prisons experienced by regular, ordinary prisoners.

Speaking more generally, this book is not about torture understood as a "regulated practice, obeying a well-defined procedure" and a technique of controlling prisoners that is not rooted in science or even a "strict judicial game" (Foucault 1979, p. 40). According to Foucault (1979, p. 34), torture as a technique is supposed to cause a certain degree of pain; "it is calculated according to detailed rules: the number of lashes of the whip, the positioning of the branding iron, the duration of the death agony on the stake or the wheel, the type of mutilation to be used." What if the applied pain is merely and exactly maintaining life in pain and not more than that? What if the pain is not calculated and not based on the legal code of pain? What if the vicious cycle of pain does not obey certain rules?

Although this book is not about torture in Iranian prisons, the pain that prisoners and their families suffer is not less (if not more) than the torture that takes place in the most hidden cells of the prisons or on the sites of public executions. In fact, prisons in Iran not only deprive prisoners of all their rights without imposing a calculated, measured degree of pain; rather, the tools of physical punishment and control over the body have not disappeared at any time in the penal system's history. Although according to Abrahamian (1999) the penal system in Iran did experience some periods of less brutal torture in prisons, albeit shortly, from the 1920s to the 1970s, especially for political prisoners, this study highlights the continuing focus on prisoners' bodies regardless of the short periods of the reformation or modernization of the penal code in Iran, whether during the Qajar reign, Pahlavi reign, or the Islamic Revolution.

Further, it was not my intention to present power as merely repressive in Iranian prisons. The spark of the so-called rehabilitation programs in the so-called prisons play a role in transforming inmates, though the impacts have been neither significant nor permanent (in one case reported in the book, only 3 prisoners participate in such programs out of 400).[1] Also, it was not my intention to ignore or deny the agency of prisoners portraying them as mere victims of the system. The irregular and unconscious interventions of prisoners help them regulate daily social life in their own desired way, which might be either compliant[2] or resistant.[3] Additionally, at any given historical moment, even though torture was the most frequently applied technique in the so-called prisons, some other technologies were also tried from time to time. Although in the process of controlling prisoners in Iranian prisons, whether in the Qajar, Pahlavi, or Islamic period, torture was the most available technology, a variety of other (sometimes contradictory) technologies for governing the prison population could nevertheless be identified.

In the very first days of the Islamic Revolution in 1979, educating and training the prisoners became prominent in prisons, something that had never occurred previously. The objective of this radical change was nested

---

[1] *"In our section, there were 400 prisoners, and fewer than 10 prisoners attended the program. In fact, from those 10 prisoners, just three of them came to the program every week, and the rest of them came rarely. Prisoners are not well-informed about the principles of the program unless they attend the class. In fact, making different rumors and jokes about NA holds some prisoners back from attending this program. We made a joke about the NA meetings and the members in the prison. Instead of Narcotics Anonymous, we called them Soldier Anonymous. I did not attend any NA meetings in the prison as I was afraid of being sent to the forced labor camp. Some prisoners heard of NA's influence in quitting drugs, and thus they decided to attend the sections"* (Male participant, seven years of incarceration) (see page 111).

[2] *"We protect each other from being bullied or assaulted by other groups in the prison. Also, we are emotionally attached to each other. We cook on the weekend with each other. Sometimes we borrow some things from our family members in the familial group." "I was a mother of some young girls in the prison, and I always encouraged them to read the Quran and be positive. I tried to protect them. We had emotional ties"* (Female participant, seven years of incarceration) (see page 121).

[3] *"Five years ago, a prison's warden decided to abandon drugs in the prison; there were a lot of protests against this decision and a lot of people were killed. Then, they did not ever abandon drugs. They found out that prisoners are more manageable by using drugs than without them"* (Male participant, seven years of incarceration) (see page 101).

in the project of turning prisons into educational institutions in which prisoners were expected to learn the elements of good behavior. Of course, the "elements of good behaviour" were based on and rooted in Islam. Therefore, according to Rejali (1994, p. 119), "prisoners are educated through what they say, hear, see, and do not see." Different techniques from the constant repetition of phrases such as "God is great; Khomeini is our leader," reciting phrases such as "God is great" by torturers during flogging, listening to designed and pre-planned programs through loudspeakers or TVs while encouraging repenting, to broadcasting religious speeches were targeted at the body and spirit of prisoners and could be considered as "tutelary torture" (Rejali 1994, p. 121). There is no period of time in history for which I can claim that power was either productive or repressive, and I cannot name a specific period in history when only one technique of power was applied. A combination of multiple techniques was always used to control the prisoners and prisons; however, the dominance of one of them, torture, constitutes a constant in Iran's penal history.

Despite significant differences between prisons for men and women, there is one in common, torture (see Table 5.1). It is ironic that prisons even when equipped with the primary rehabilitation facilities, from Narcotics Anonymous' programs to social skill classes, failed to get rid of the mere torture as the foundation of the Iranian prison. It comes as no surprise that prisons, which have never succeeded in providing prisoners

Table 5.1 Differences between prisons for men and women

Prisons for men	Prisons for women
Gangs	No gangs
No Familial groups	Familial groups
Importance of social capital (e.g. having contact with family and friends outside prison) on men's status in prison	Social capital outside of prison is less important
No children inside prison	Children are allowed inside prison
Not common	Prevalence of making rumors as punishment
Prevalence of physical violence	Not common
Not common	Verbal violence

with proper rehabilitation programs, use the children and drugs as escape paths. While the children along with their imprisoned mothers suffer extreme dehumanizing pain, their experiences are trivialized. The penitentiary administration abuses them, due to the lack of other strategies, making them a tool to run prisons and to keep the situation under control. In these circumstances, the false assumption that the children in prisons benefit from mother-child bonding should be avoided.

As it is for the children in prison, the lack of attention toward the hazardous effects of the availability of drugs in prisons leads to many flawed assumptions, such as the belief that methadone treatment prevents prisoners from seeking and using hard drugs in prisons. In other words, Iranian penal strategies used to govern prisons do not rely on scientific pre-planned and pre-examined knowledge, but rather on non-expert, incidental, and circumstantial knowledge. The near absence of expert knowledge in the penal system of Iran makes it hard to acknowledge the technico-disciplinary foundation of the penal imprisonment, which aims at not just the deprivation of liberty, but rather the "technical transformation of individuals" (Foucault 1979, p. 233).

Foucault (1979, p. 16) states that "a trace of torture in the modern mechanisms of criminal justice… has not been entirely overcome, but which is enveloped, increasingly, by the non-corporal nature of the penal system." The severity of pain in the last 200 years in Iranian prisons has been reduced, albeit not significantly. Although it was not the objective of the current study to analyze changes in the Penal Code, it is noteworthy that penal severity has been reduced in the Islamic penal code in the recent decades. Nonetheless, the prison conditions have not changed significantly. Only the architectural design of prisons did. It is true that the agency of the most modern penal systems goes beyond the bodies since the inmates' soul, spirit, and lives become affected. However, targeting the body of prisoners and their families still plays a crucial role in Iranian penal system. In this sense, Iranian prisons are an element of a premodern system of governance.

The discussion of the system of governance in Iran clearly requires placing prison in a broader social context. The task of situating the institution of prison in Iran in a broader social context goes, however, beyond the scope of this book and represents a promising direction for further studies. The unfinished modernization of prison can be better understood in the context of the unfinished modernization of Iranian society[4] and more data are needed to study this link. The issue of trust illustrates this point: modern institutions need a certain level of generalized trust to operate. The level of generalized trust is critically low both in prison and society in Iran. The crisis of trust in the Islamic Republic of Iran was confirmed by the results on nationwide representative surveys. According to a World Values Survey conducted in this country in 2005, 88.7% of Iranians declared they must be careful in dealing with others. The level of generalized trust in this country, 10.5%, is two and a half times less than the average for the World Values Survey general sample (25.4%). Yet even the most recent data on trust are not readily available since Iran was not a part of the 2014 wave of the World Values Survey.[5]

References

Abrahamian, E. (1999). *Tortured Confessions: Prisons and Public Recantations in Modern Iran*. University of California Press.

Foucault, M. (1979). *Discipline and Punish: The Birth of the Prison*. Vintage.

Foucault, M. (2007). *Security, Territory, Population: Lectures at the Collège De France, 1977–78*. Springer.

Garland, D. (1986). Foucault's Discipline and Punish – An Exposition and Critique. *American Bar Foundation Research Journal, 11, 847*.

Oleinik, A. (2003). *Organized Crime, Prison and Post-Soviet Societies*. Routledge.

Rejali, D. M. (1994). *Torture and Modernity: Self, Society, and State in Modern Iran*. Westview.

[4] A similar observation was made in (Oleinik 2003) with respect to the Russian case.

[5] The 2004 wave was conducted during a short period of the "thaw," when the Judiciary Power of Islamic Republic of Iran and the Islamic Republic of Iran Prisons Organization also hosted the first International Conference on Reducing the Use of Incarceration in Tehran (June 2007).

Index[1]

[1] Note: Page numbers followed by 'n' refer to notes.

N. R. Anaraki, *Prison in Iran*, Palgrave Studies in Prisons and Penology,
https://doi.org/10.1007/978-3-030-57169-6

W

Z

The manufacturer's authorised representative in the EU is Springer
Nature Customer Service Centre GmbH, Europaplatz 3, 69115 Heidelberg,
Germany. If you have any concerns regarding our products, please
contact ProductSafety@springernature.com

Printed and bound by CPI Group (UK) Ltd, Croydon, CR0 4YY
30/09/2026
02225453-0001